MY Magical PRESCHOOL WORKBOOK

by Jacy Corral

This book belongs to:

. . . .

Want free goodies?!

Email us at

modernkidpress@gmail.com

Title the email "My Magical Preschool Workbook!"
and we'll send some goodies your way!

Follow us on Instagram!
@modernkidpress

Questions & Customer Service:
Email us at modernkidpress@gmailcom!

Trace the
Lines

You can do it!

Horizontal Lines

Horizontal Lines

Vertical Lines

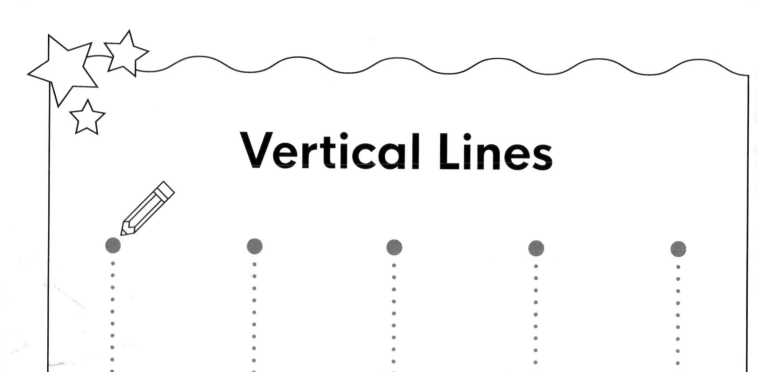

Vertical Lines

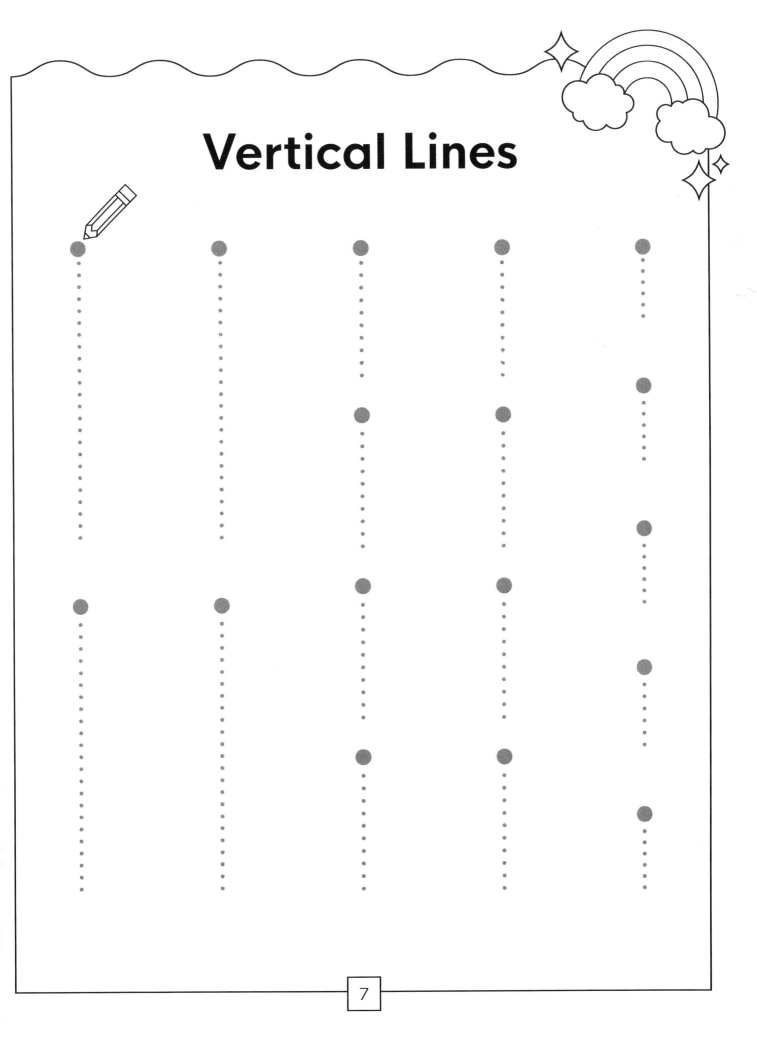

Zigzag Lines

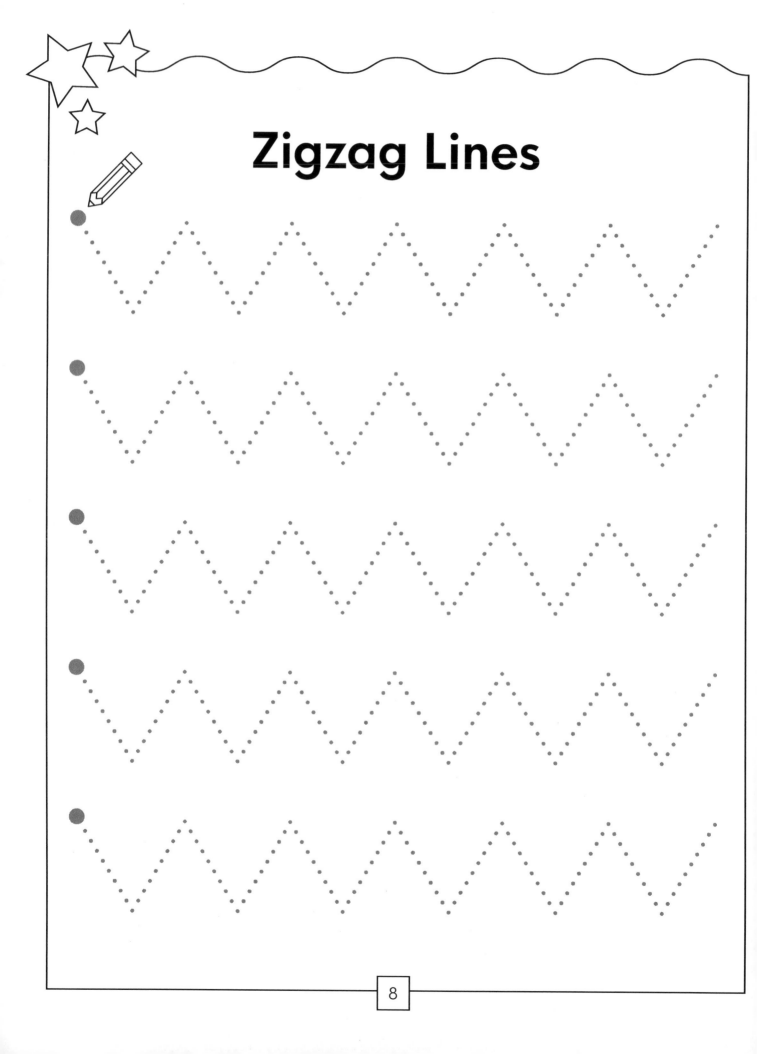

Zigzag Lines

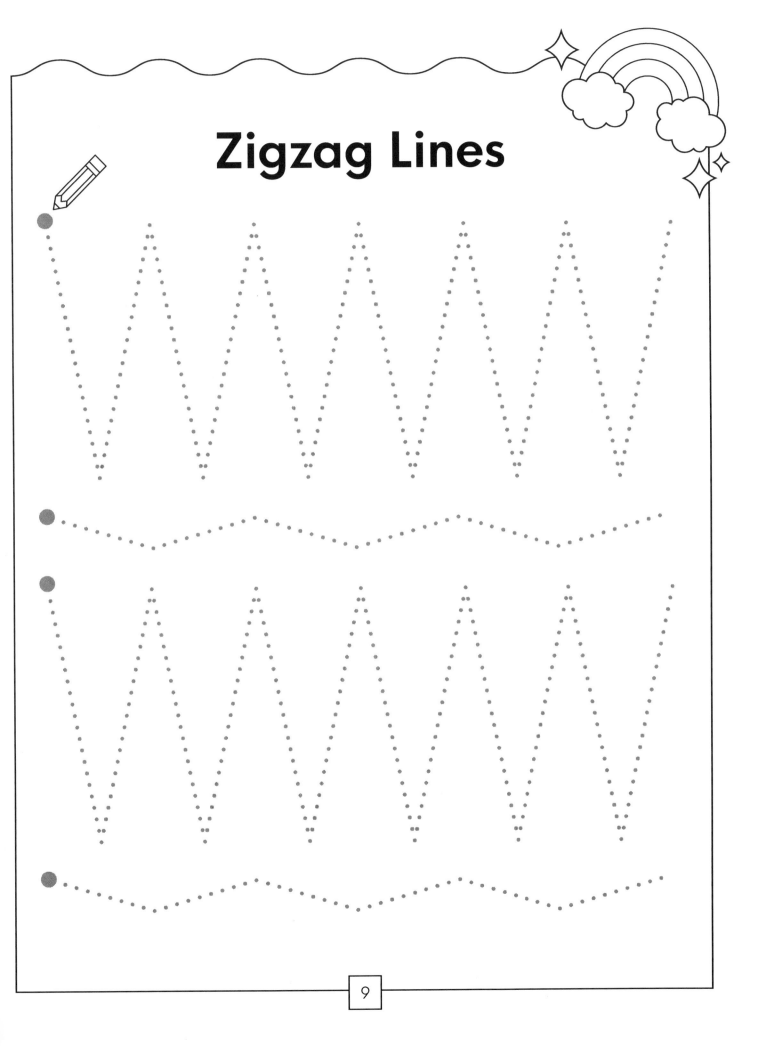

Square Zigzag Lines

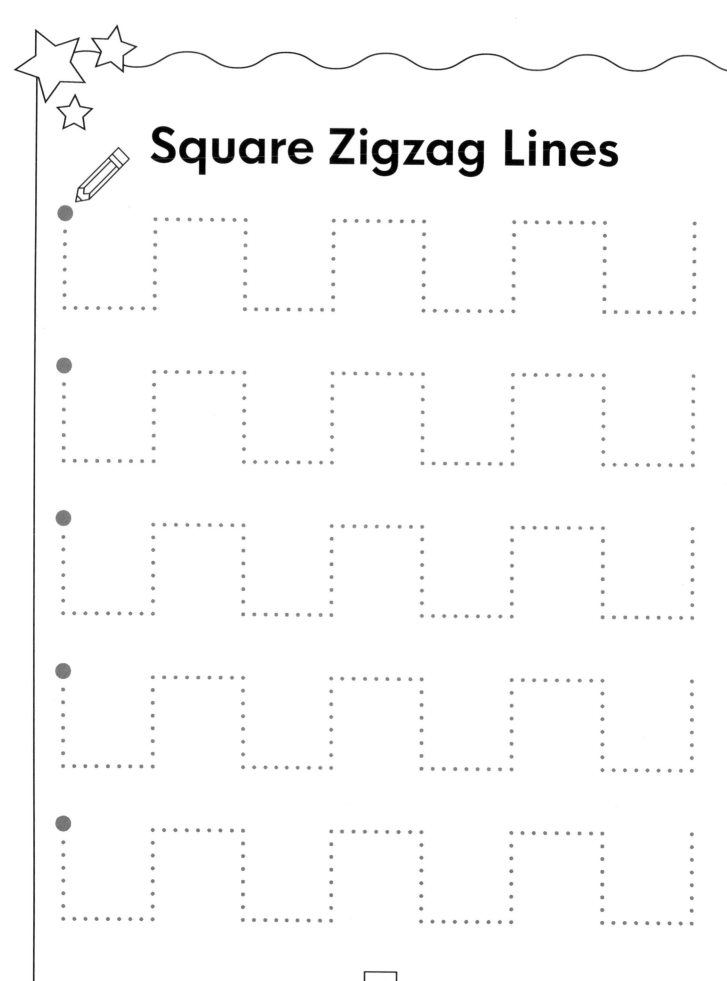

Square Zigzag Lines

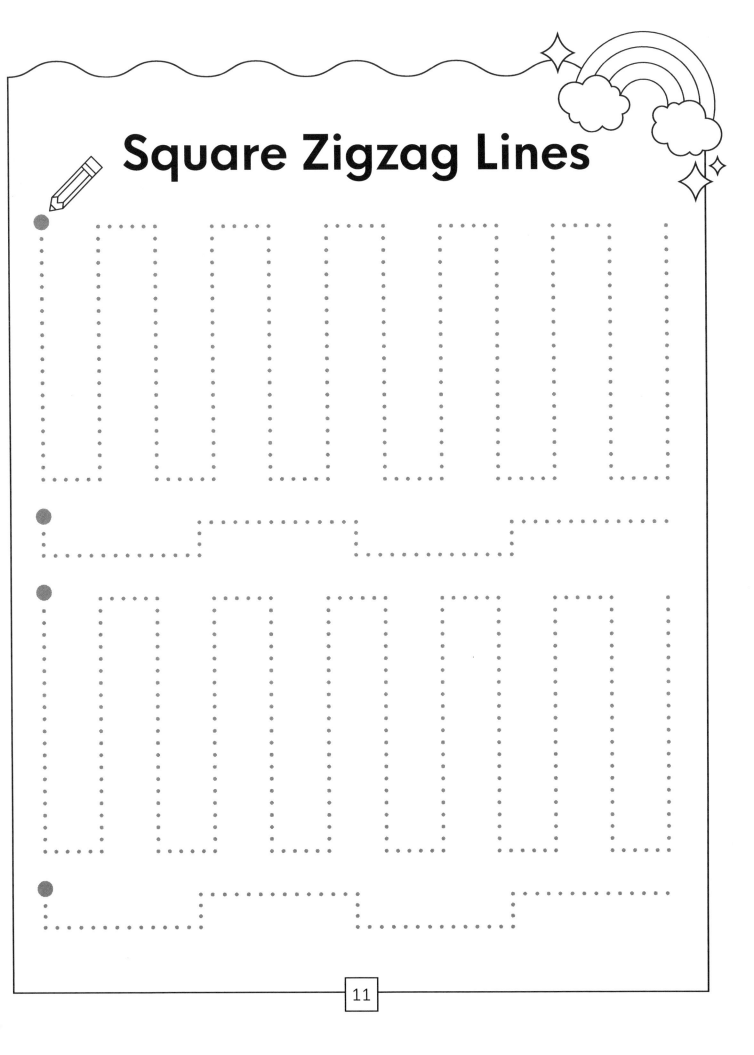

Wavy Lines

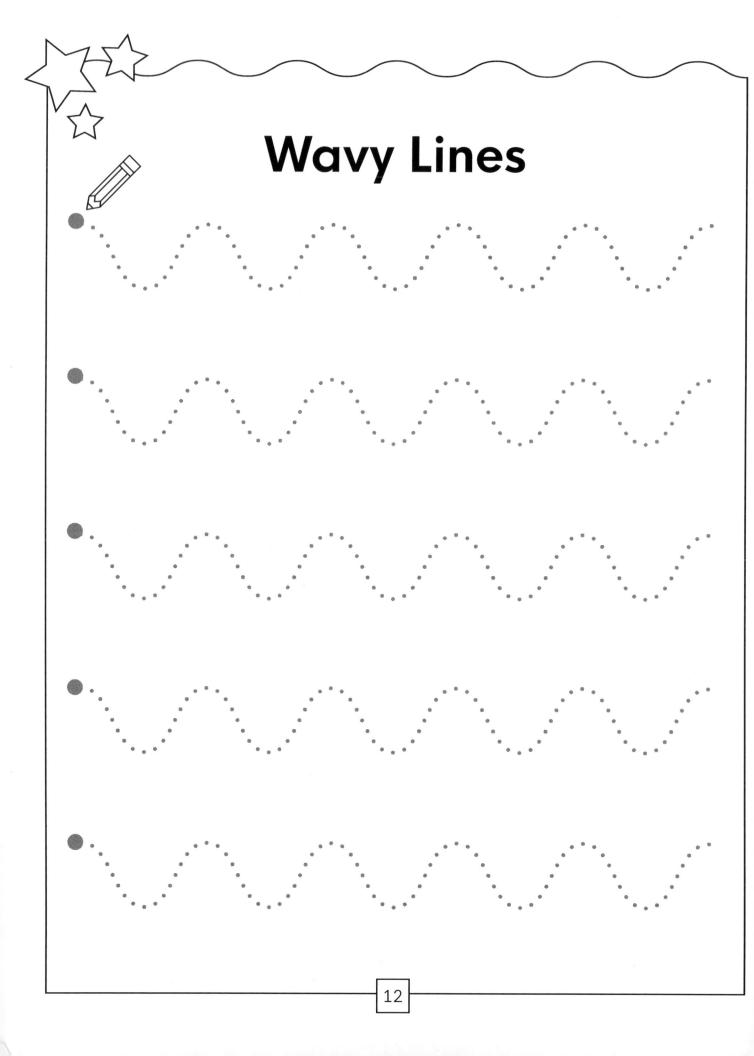

Wavy Lines

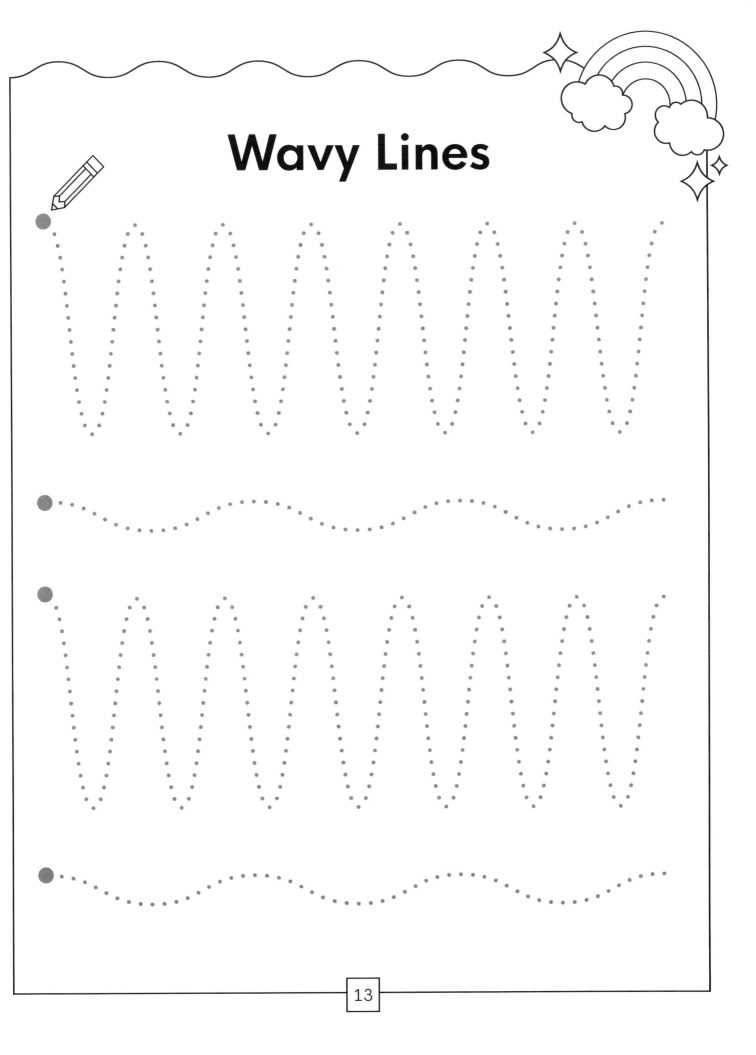

Loopy Lines

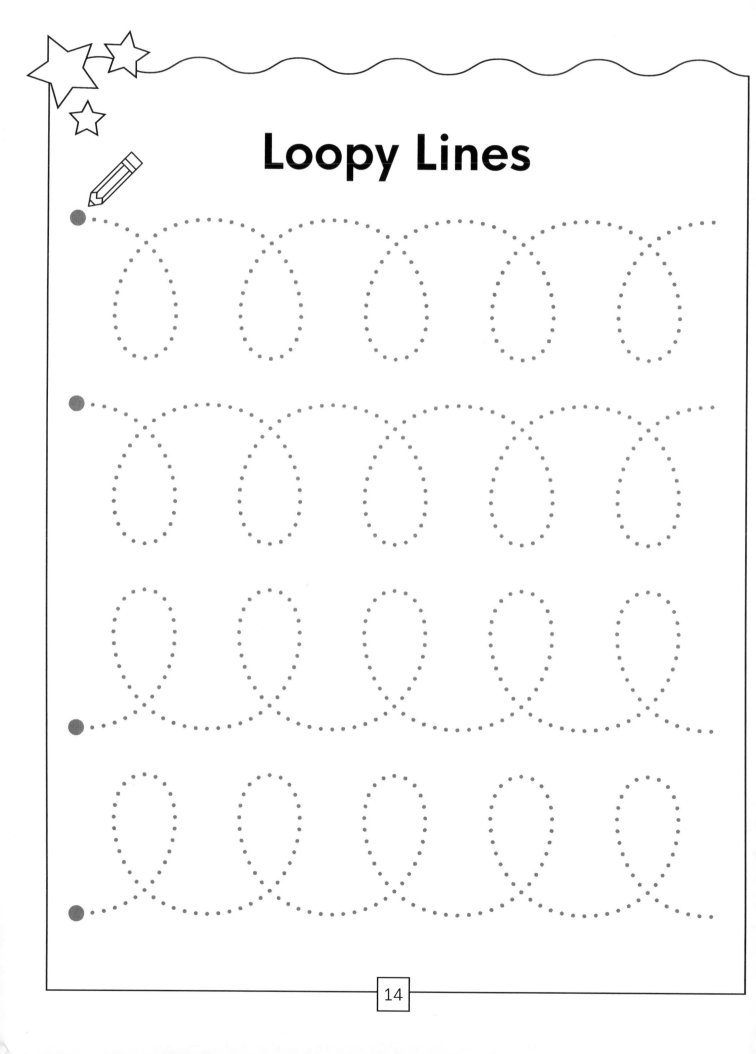

Loopy Lines

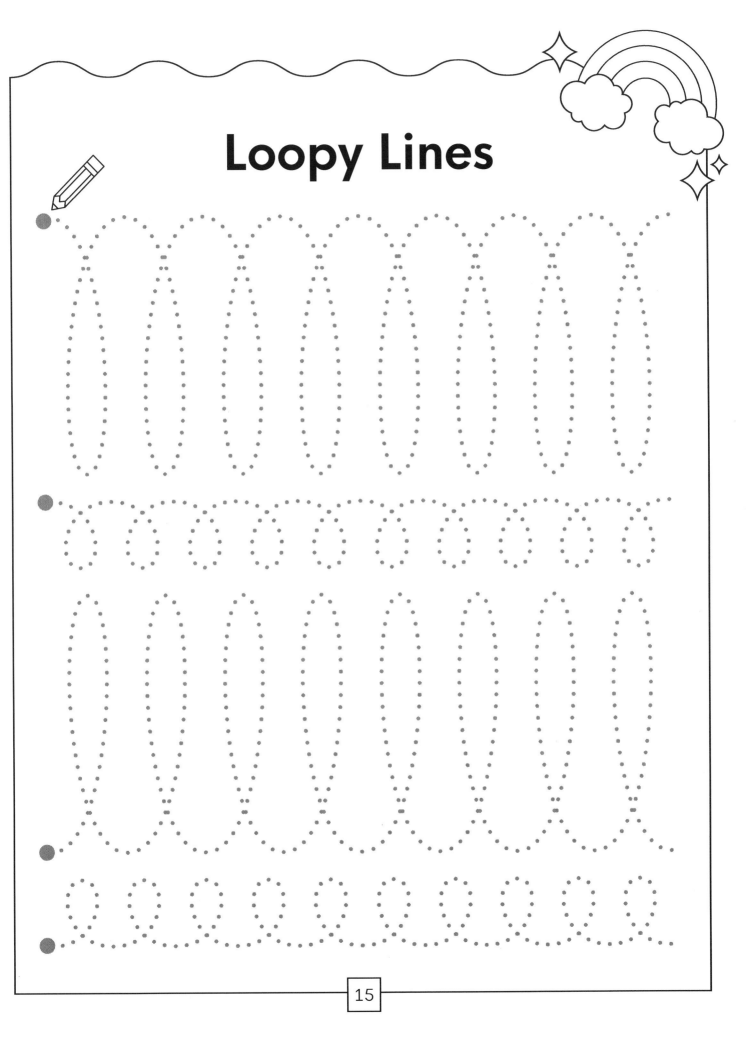

Spiral Lines

First, try drawing a spiral from the outside.

Then try it from the middle!

Spiral Lines

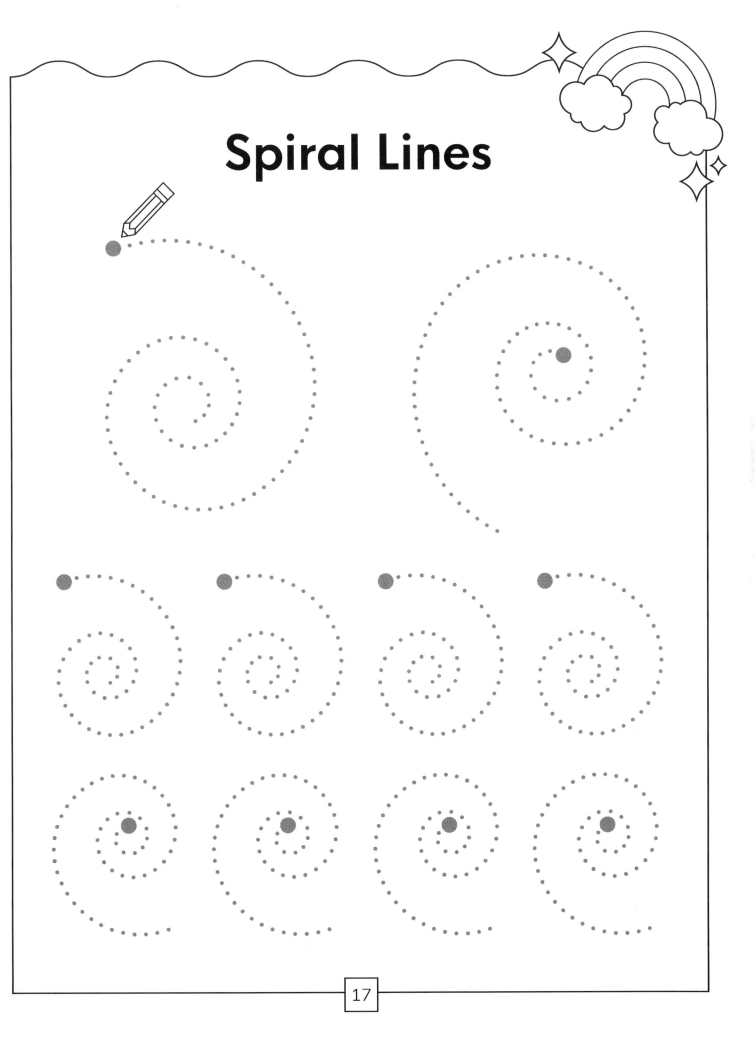

Grid Lines

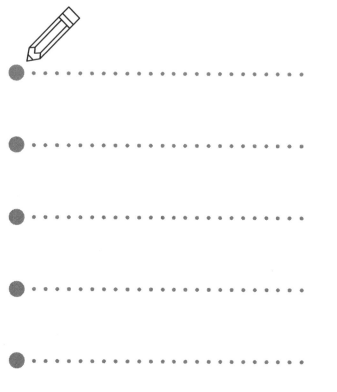

First, pratice drawing vertical and horizontal lines one more time.

Grid Lines

Now, put them together! Start with the vertical lines, then add the horizontal.

Trace the Lines

Connect the Dots with Different Kinds of Lines

Connect the Dots with Different Kinds of Lines

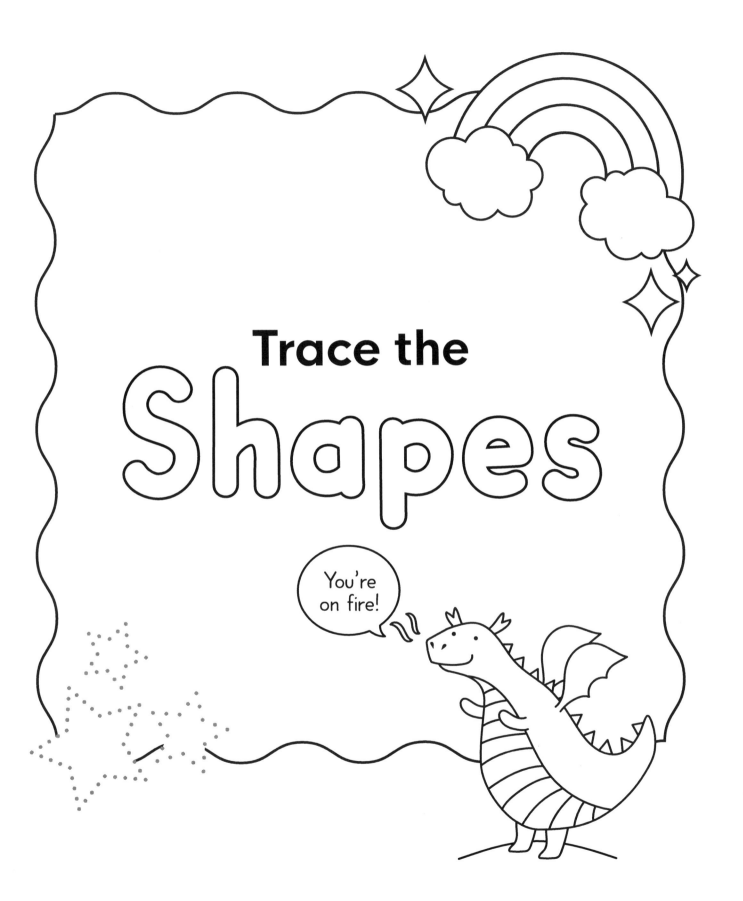

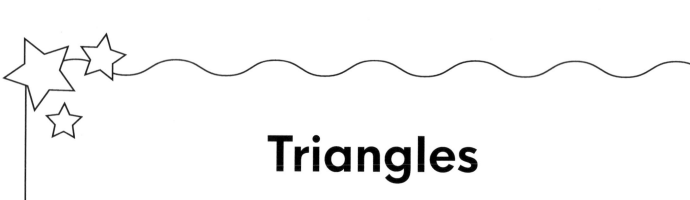

Triangles

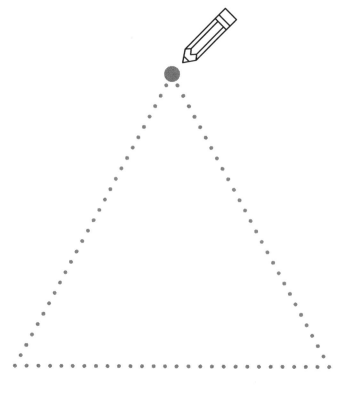

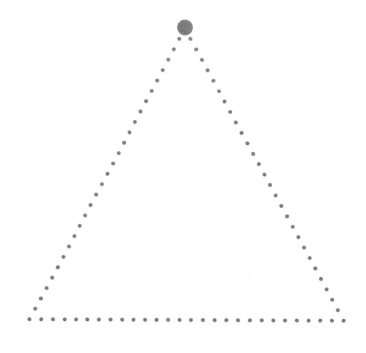

Triangles

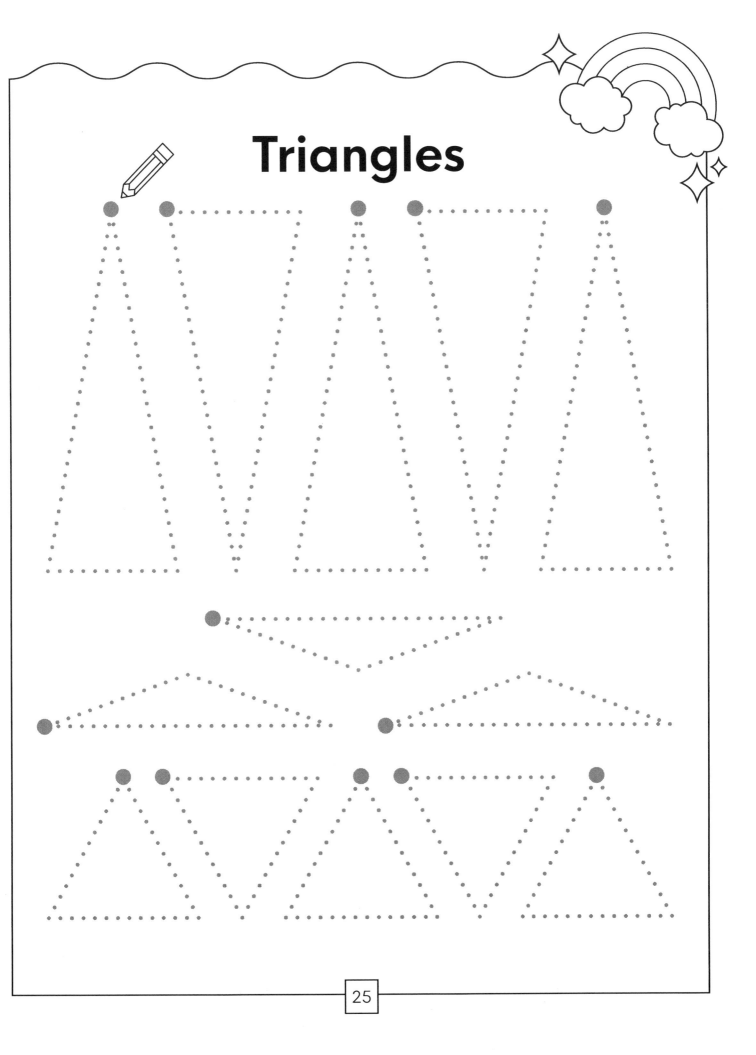

Squares

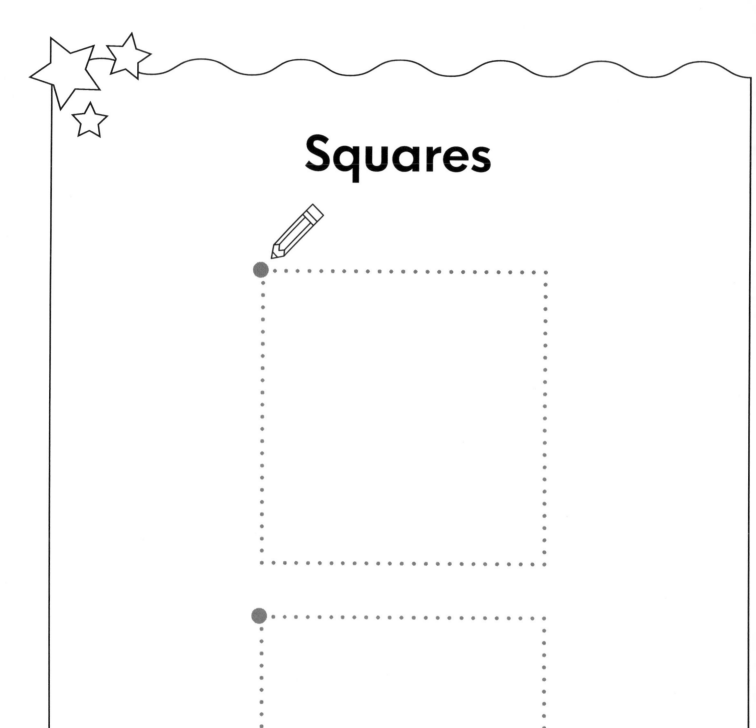

Squares

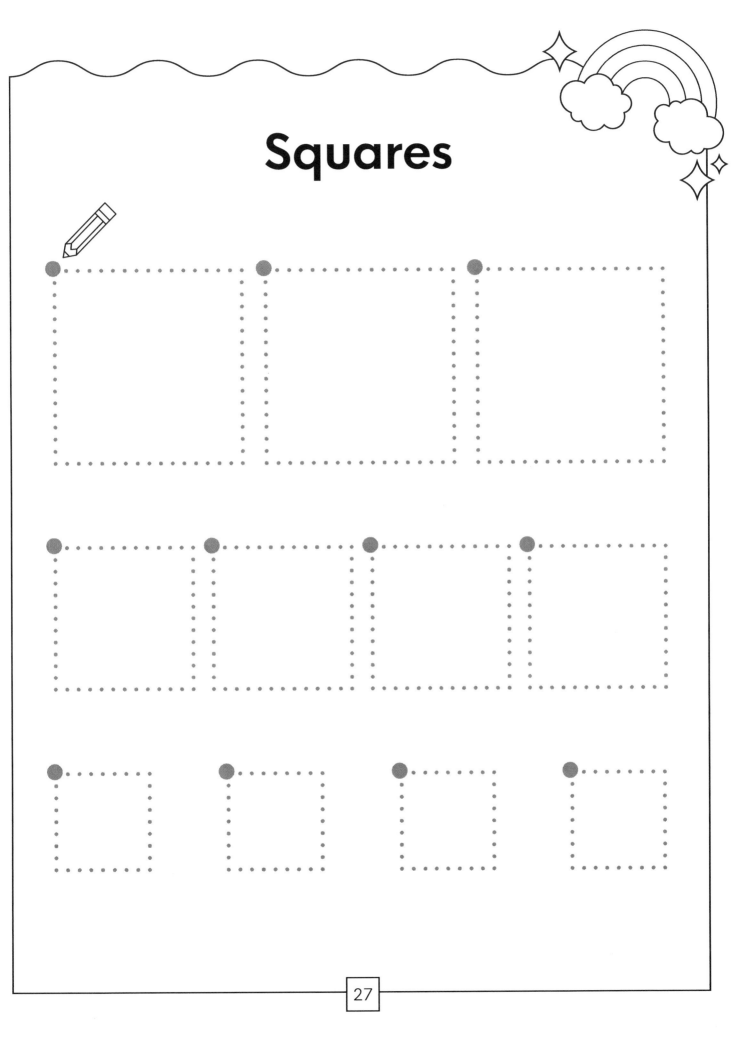

Parallelograms

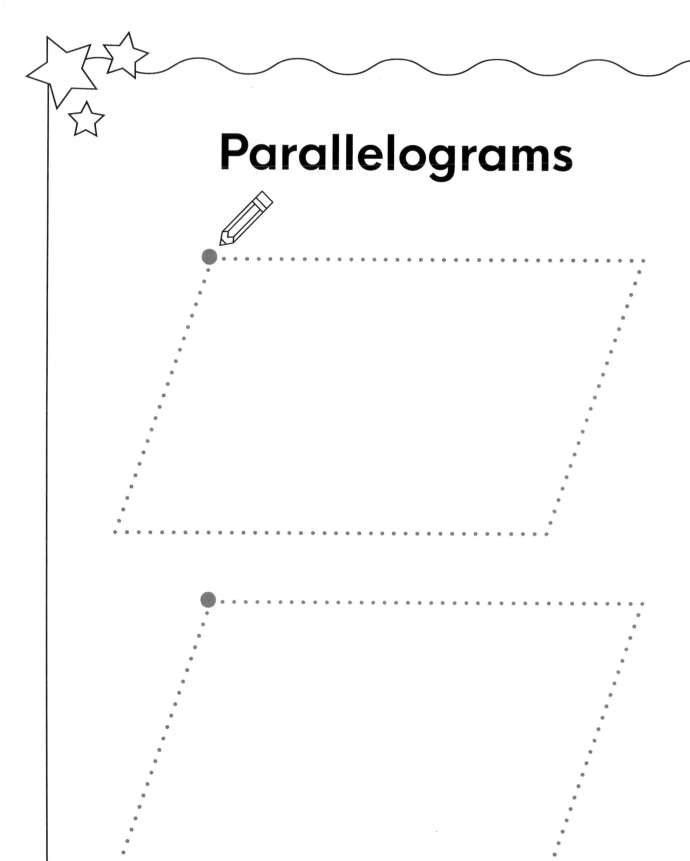

Parallelograms

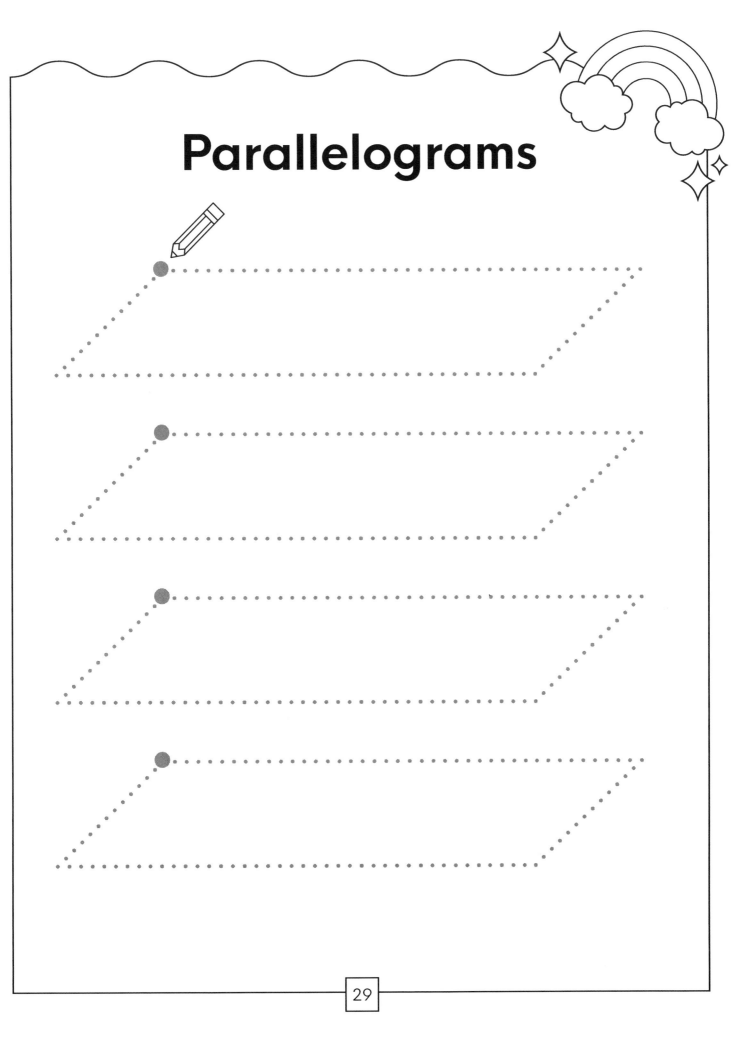

Diamonds

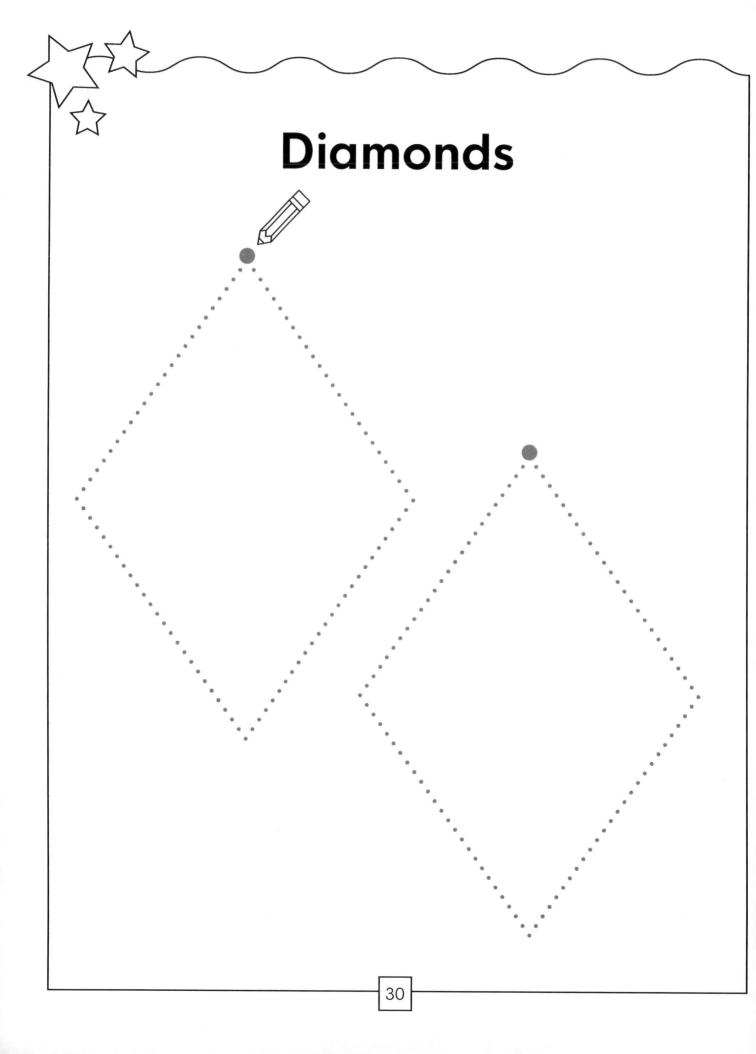

Diamonds

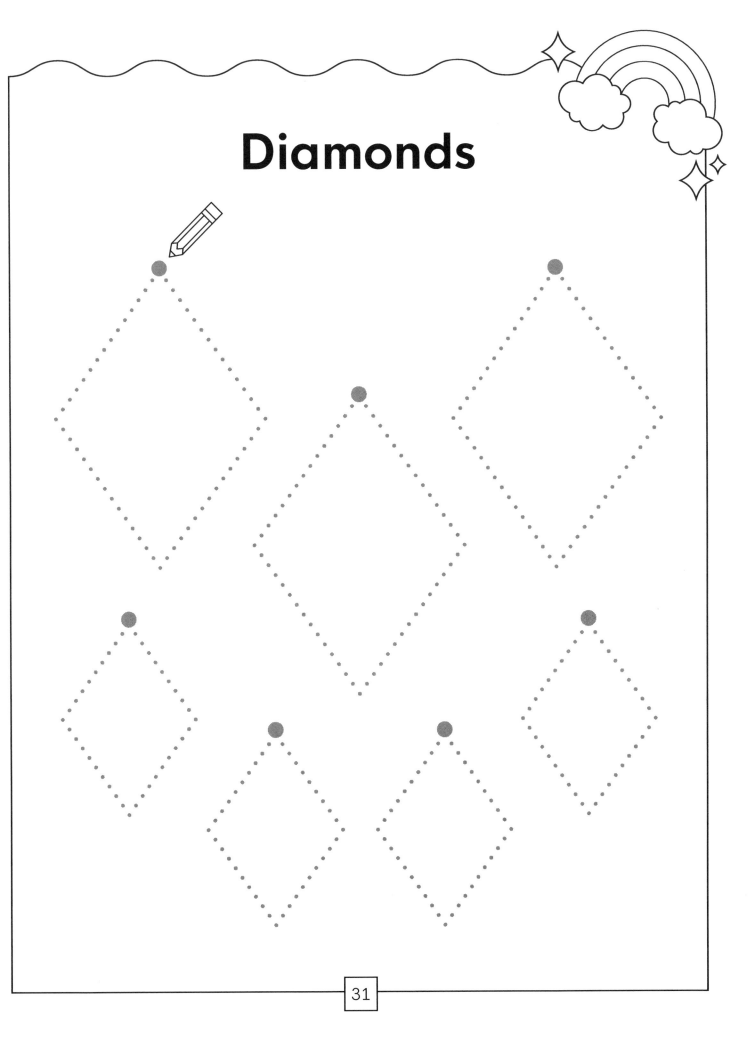

Pentagons

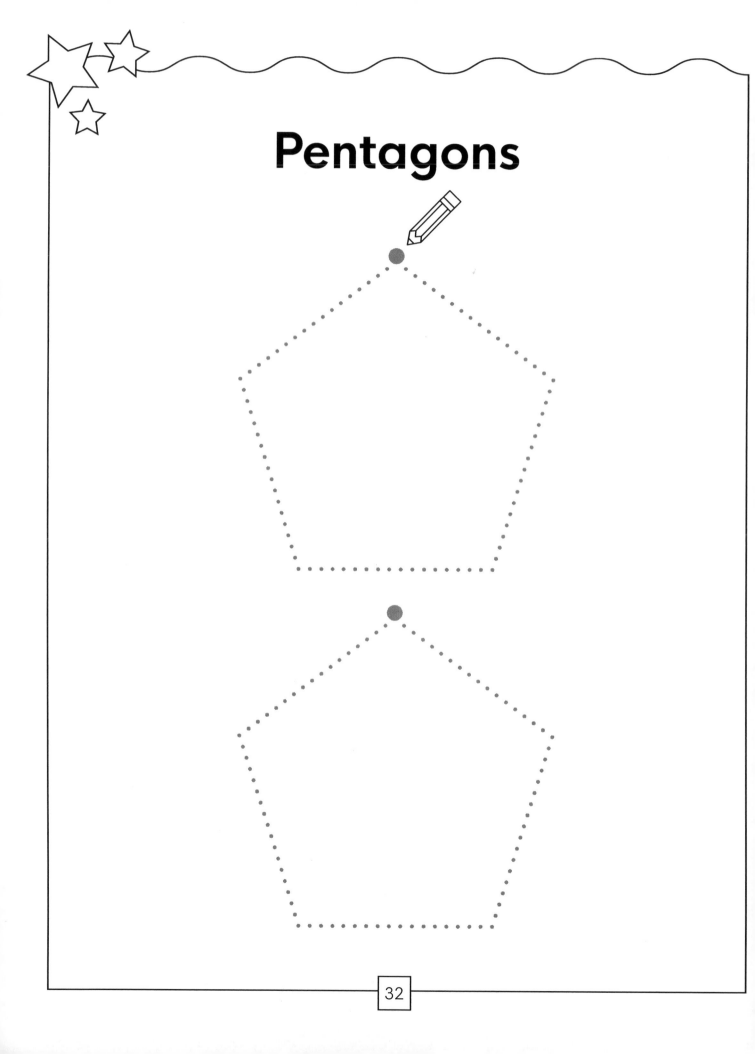

Pentagons

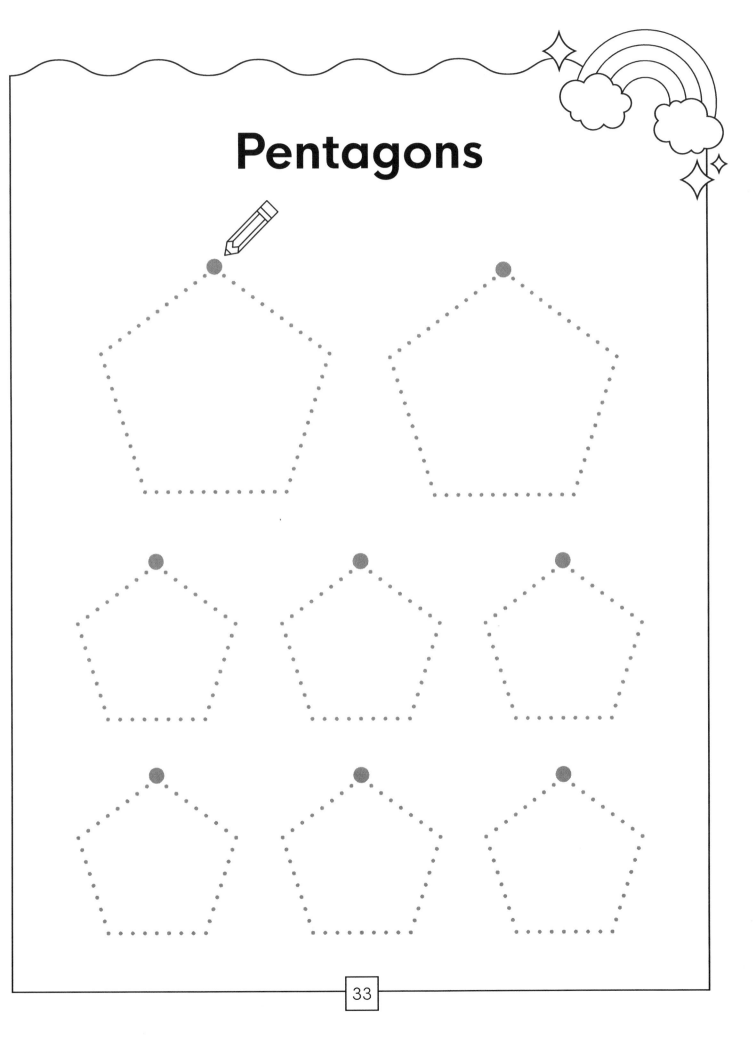

Circles

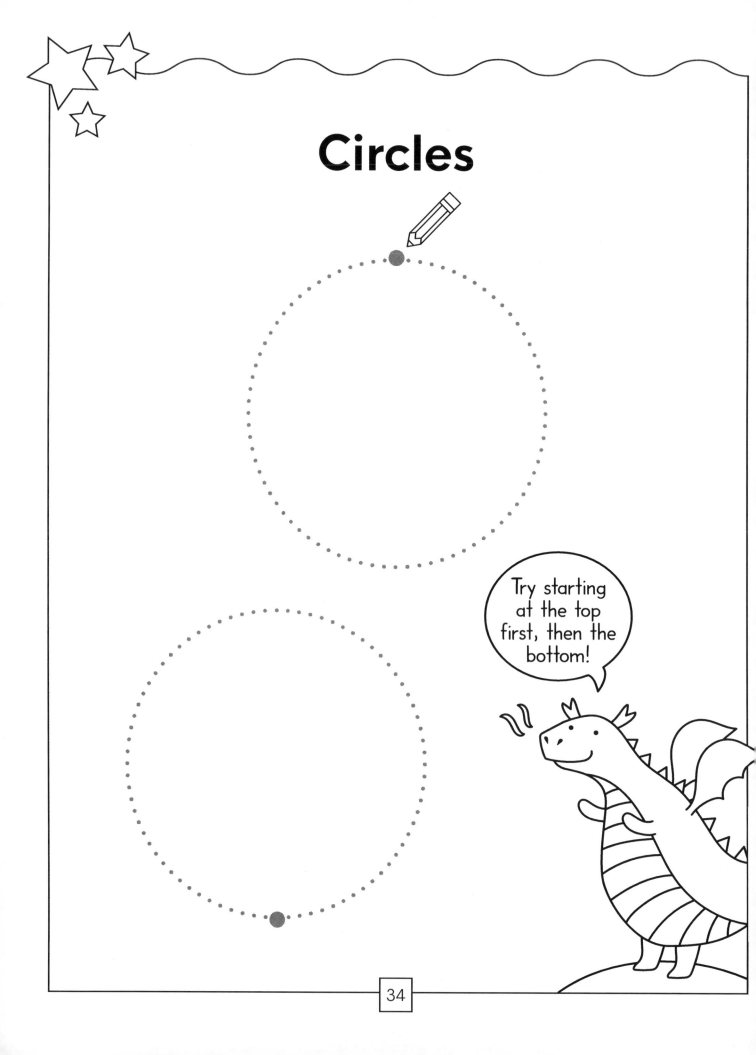

Try starting at the top first, then the bottom!

Circles

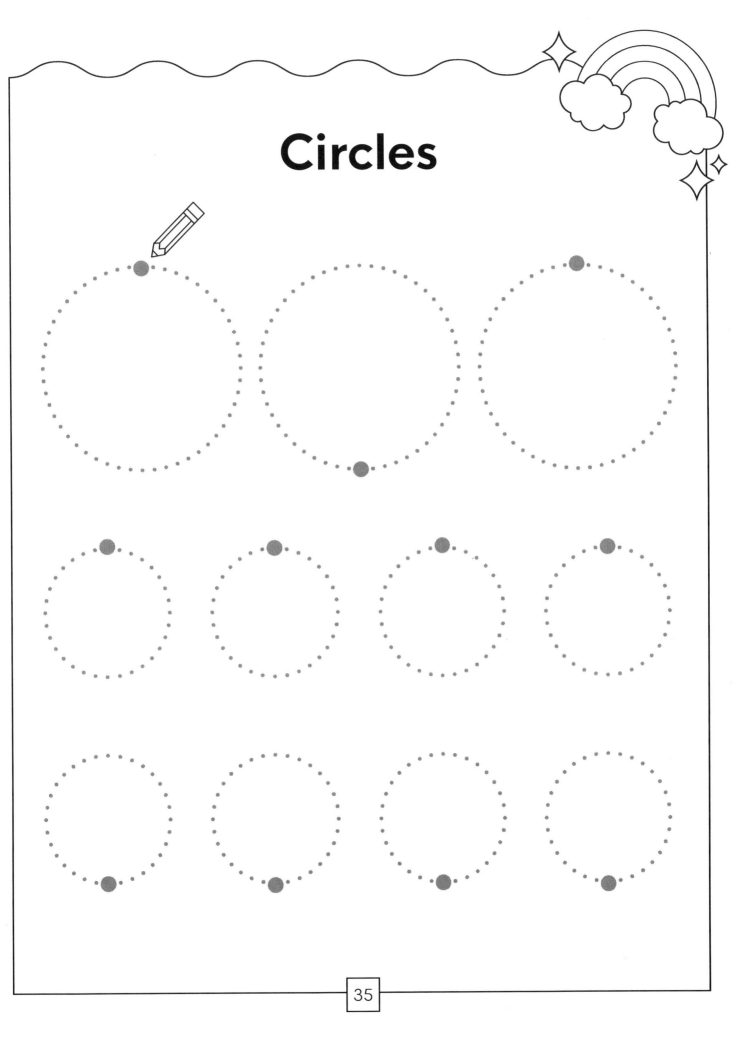

Ovals

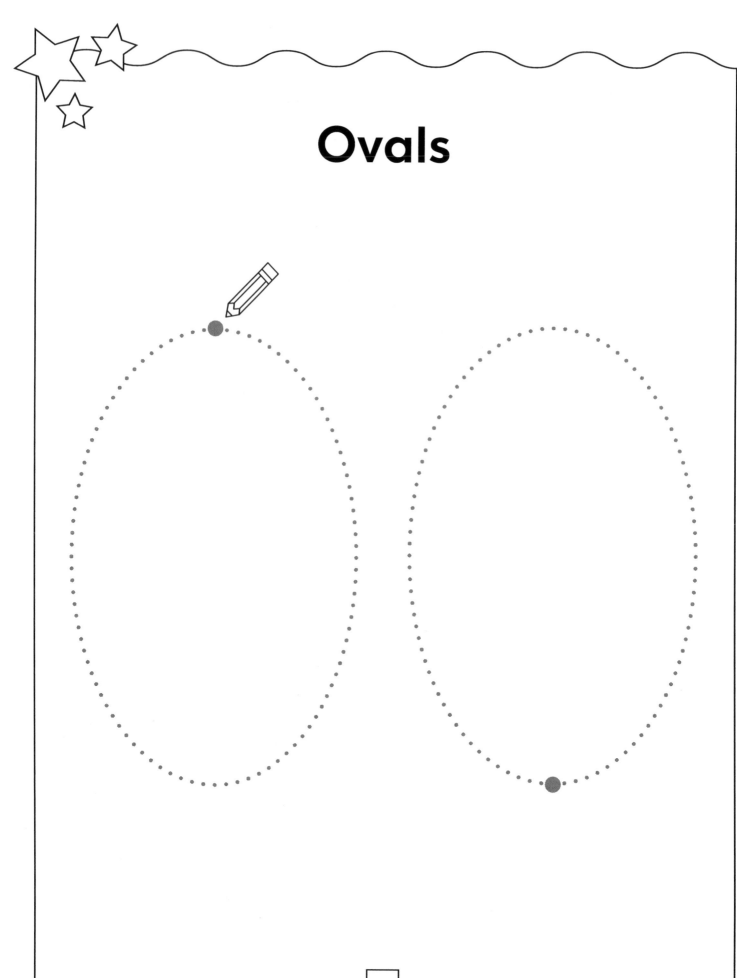

Ovals

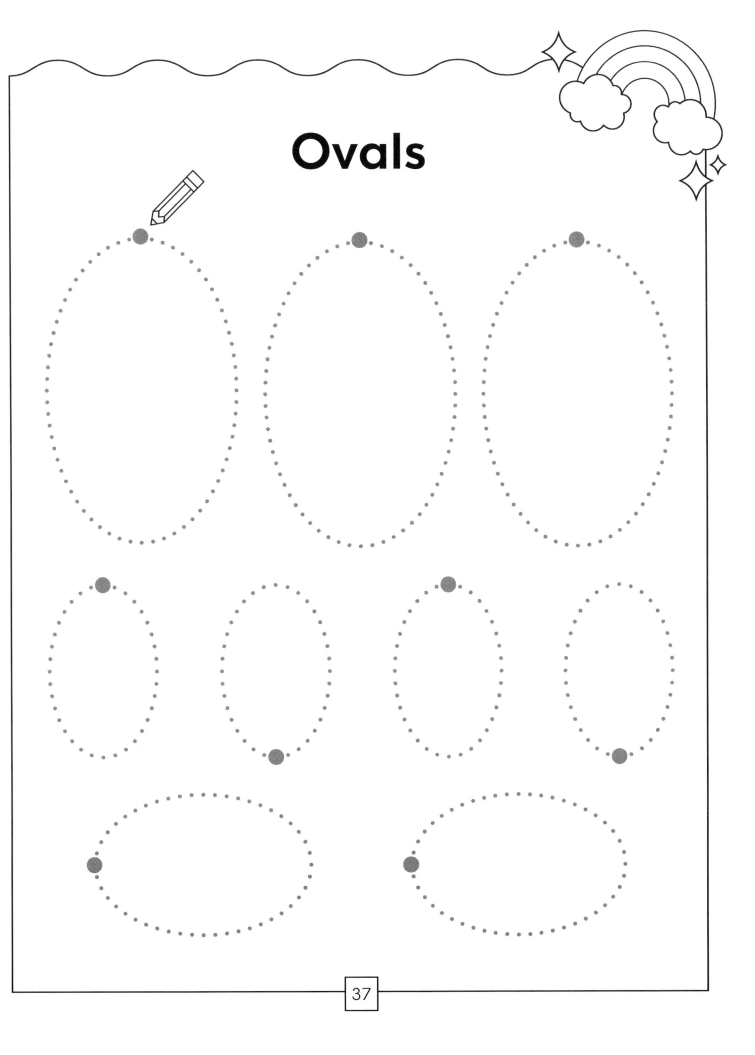

Semi-Circle

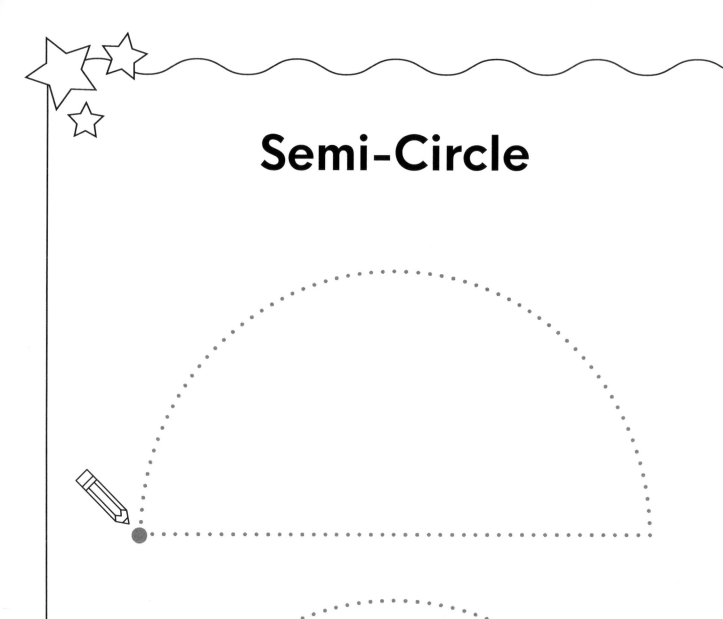

Semi-Circle

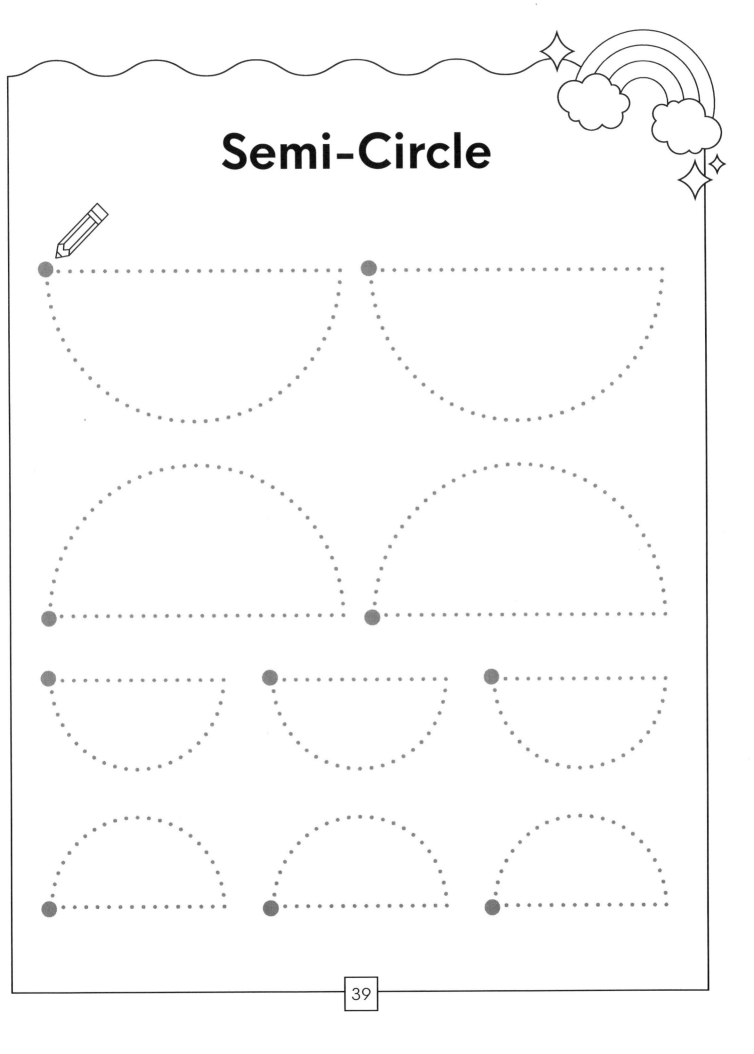

Crescents

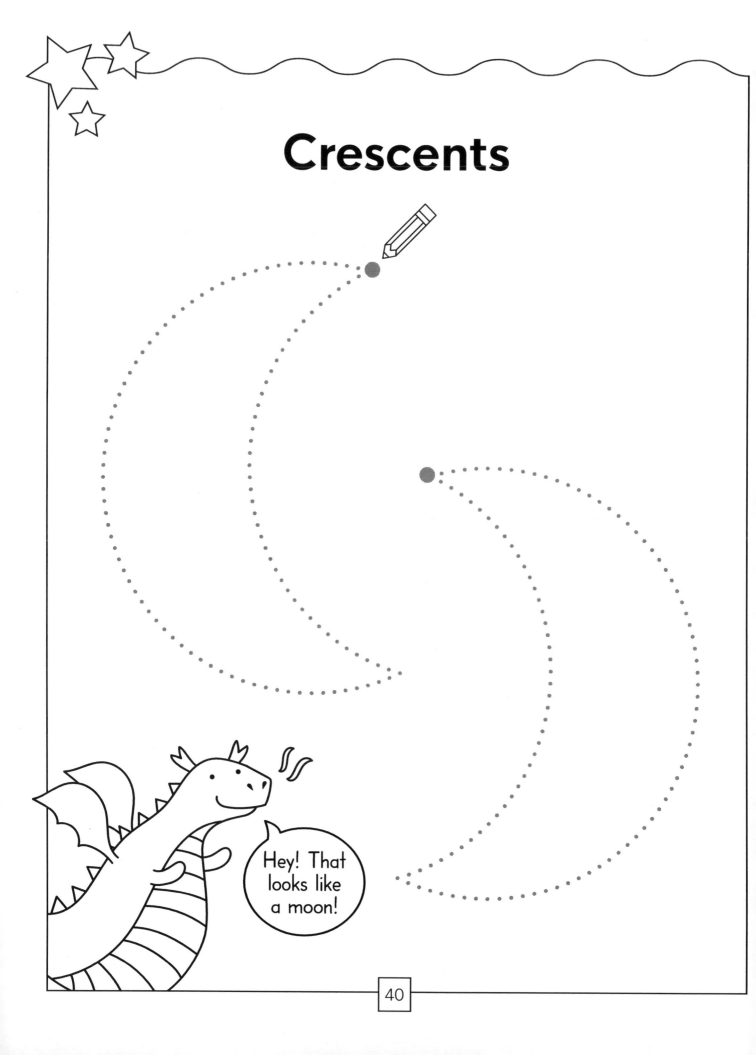

Crescents

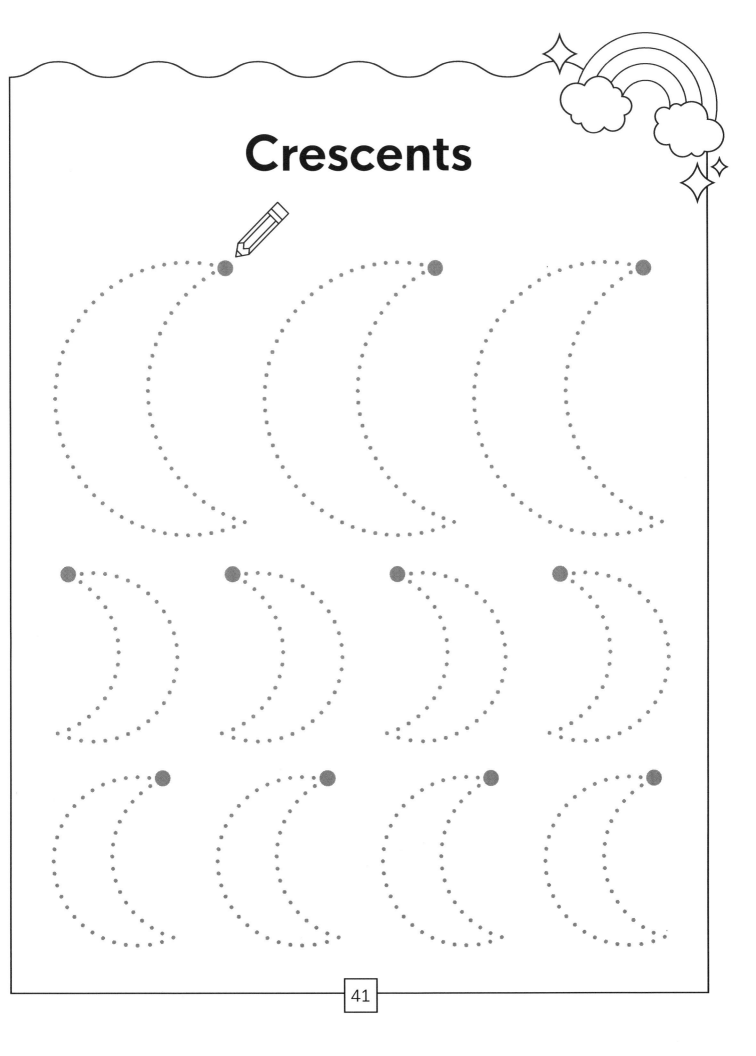

Stars

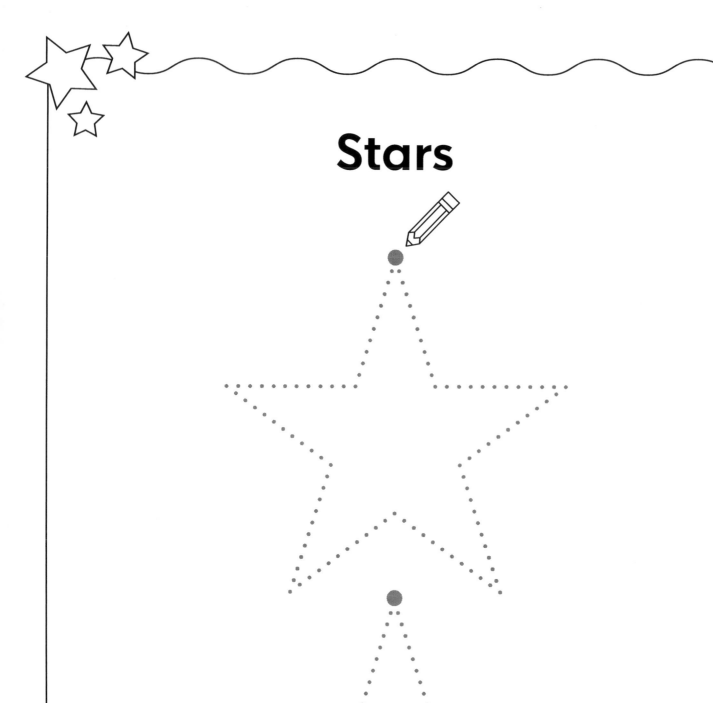

Stars

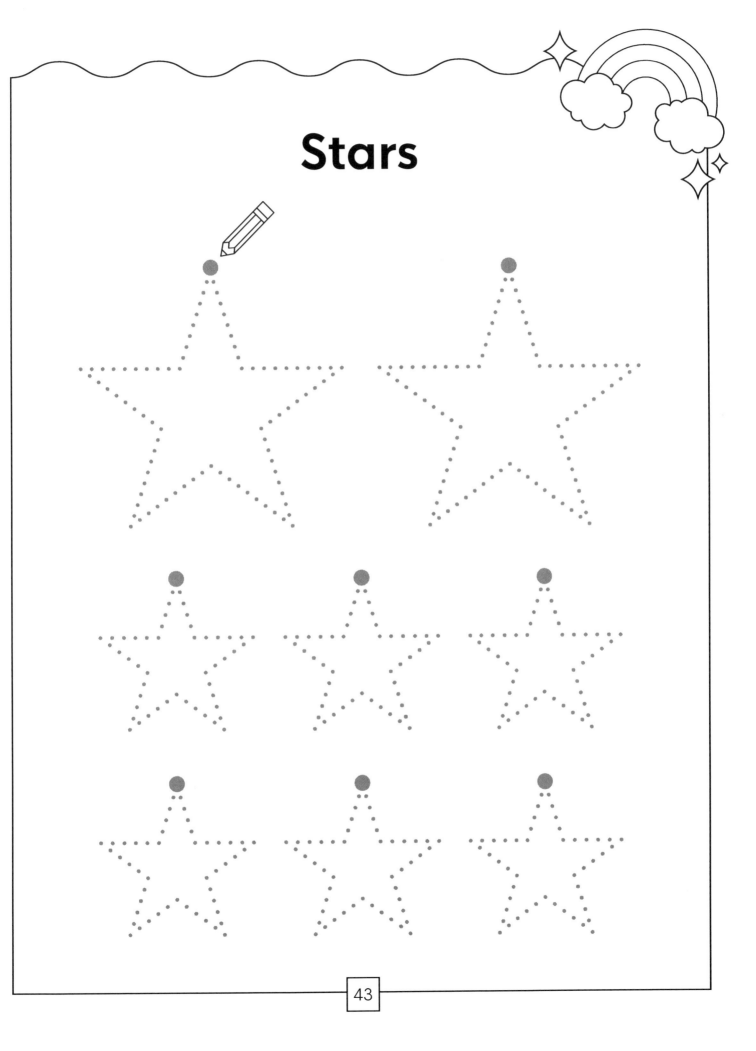

Hearts

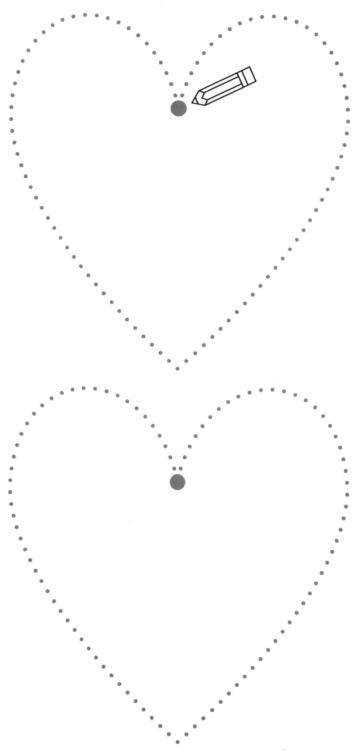

Hearts

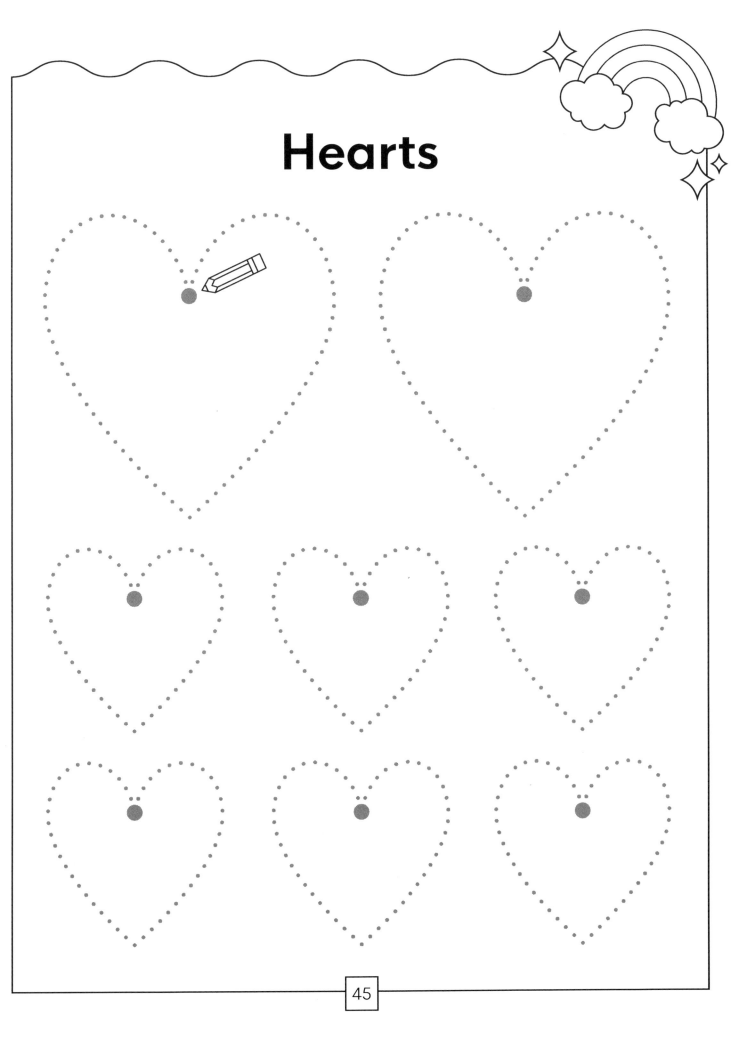

Rain Drops

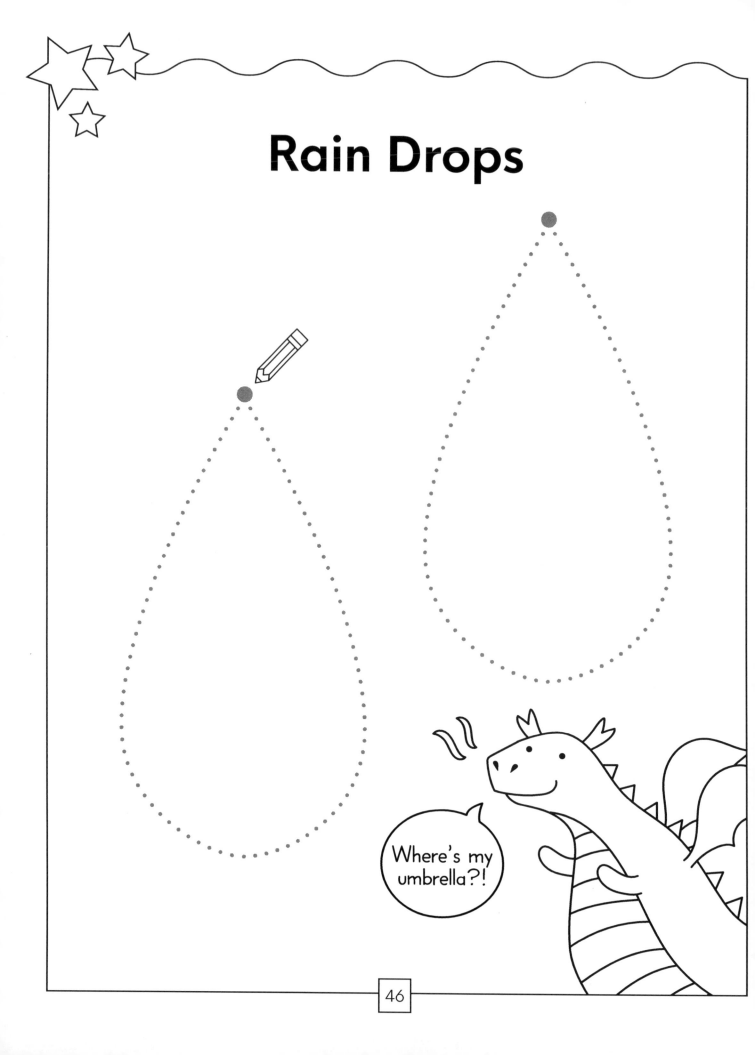

Where's my umbrella?!

Rain Drops

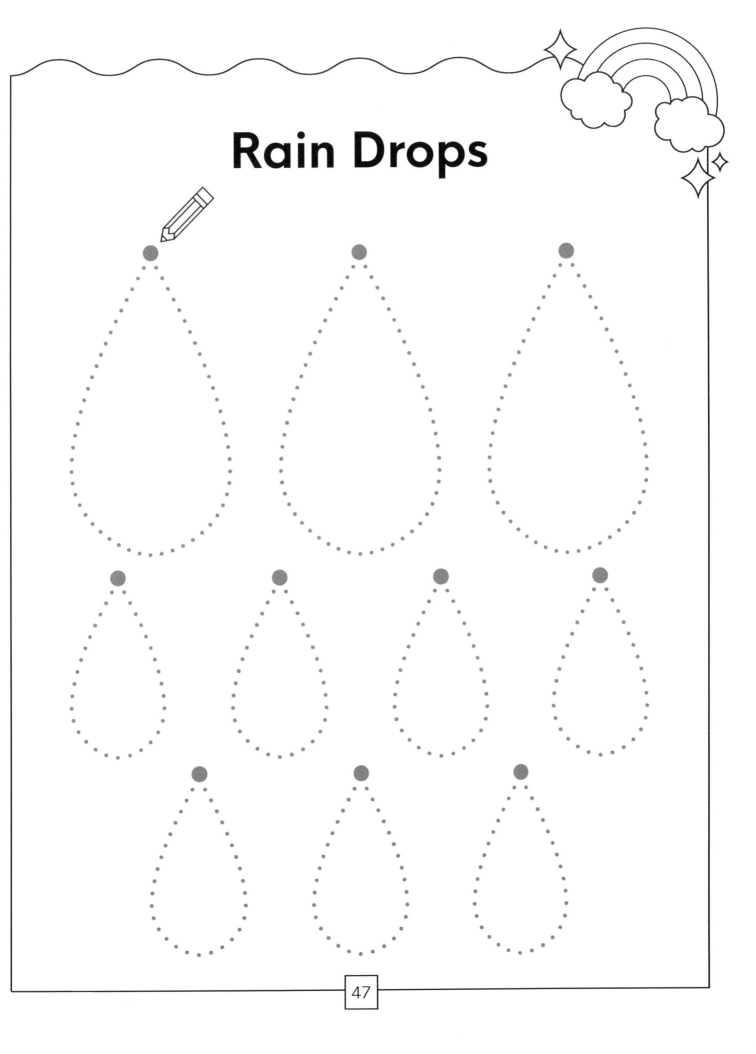

Turn the Shapes
Into Pictures

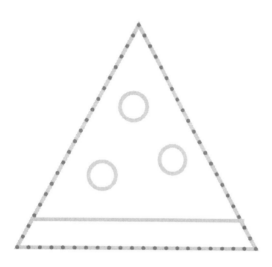 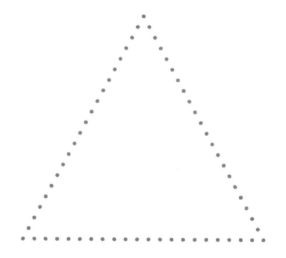

Turn the Shapes
Into Pictures

Turn the Shapes Into Pictures

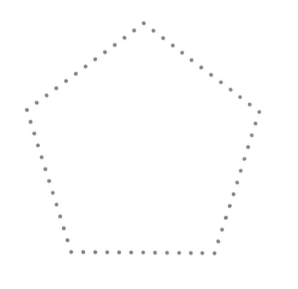
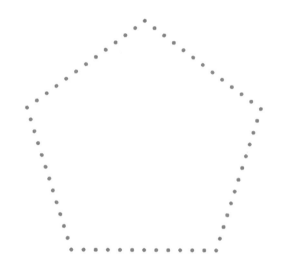

Turn the Shapes Into Pictures

Turn the Shapes Into Pictures

Sun

Flower

Butterfly

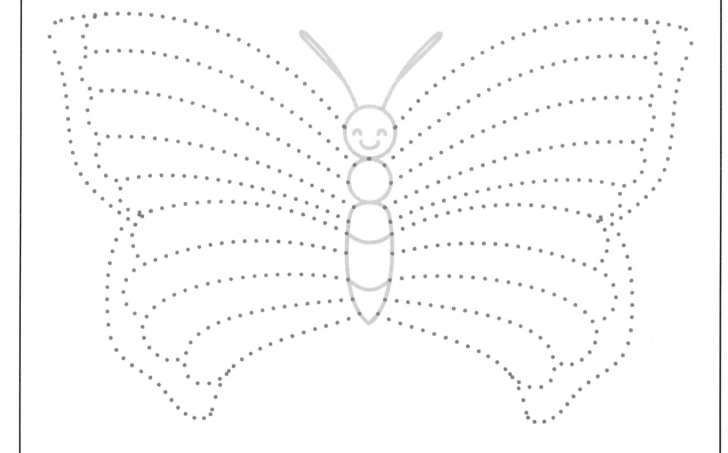

Story Book

Draw the cover of **your** story!

Mirror

Wand

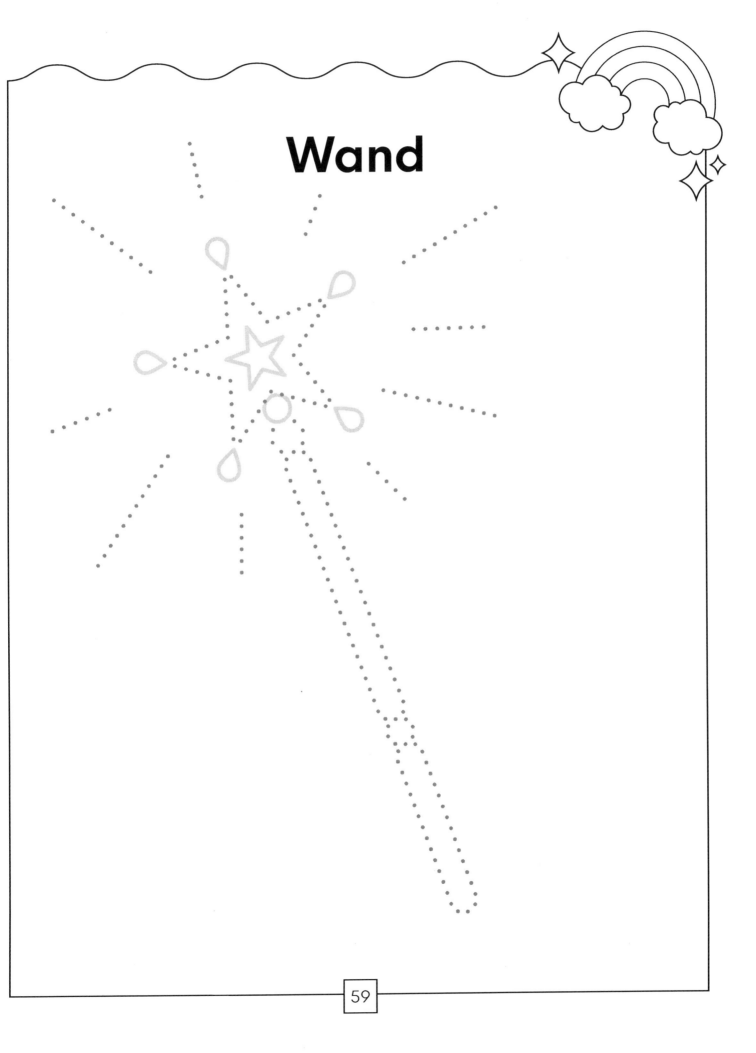

Princess Hat

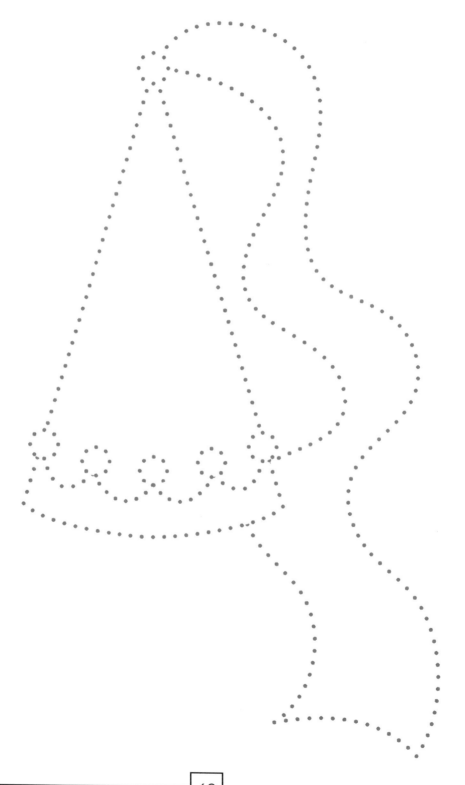

Crown

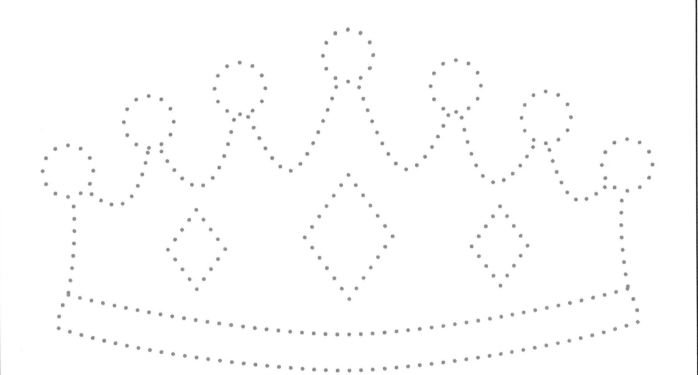

Sword

Shield

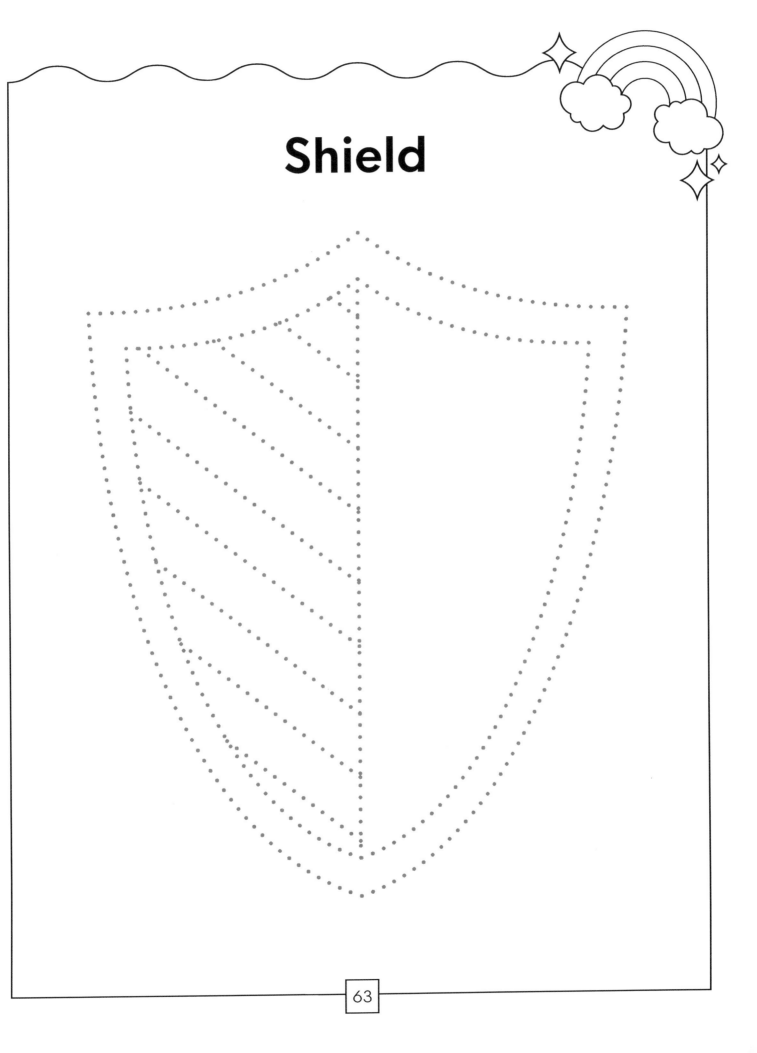

Rainbow

Ring

Ice Cream

Gems

Castle

Princess

Knight

Dragon

Fairy

Trace the
Letters

I believe in you!

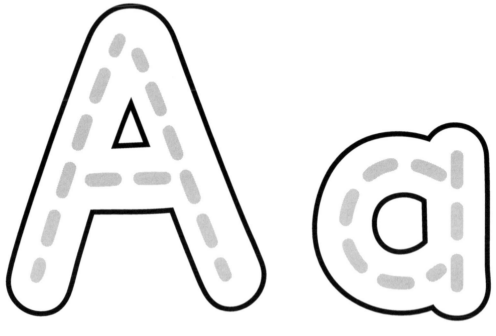

Cc

E e

E E E E

e e e e e

G g

G G G G G

g g g g g

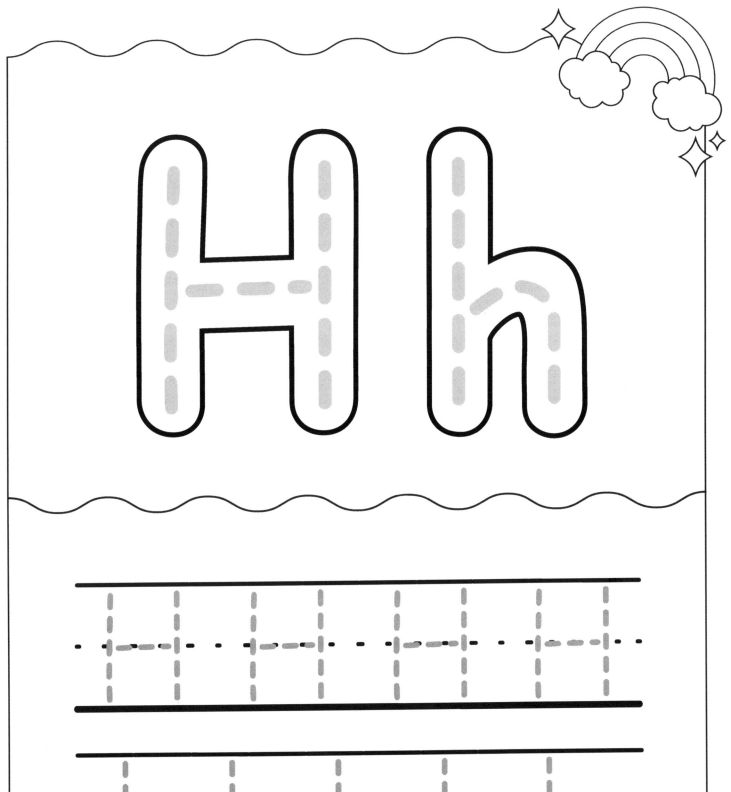

I i

Kk

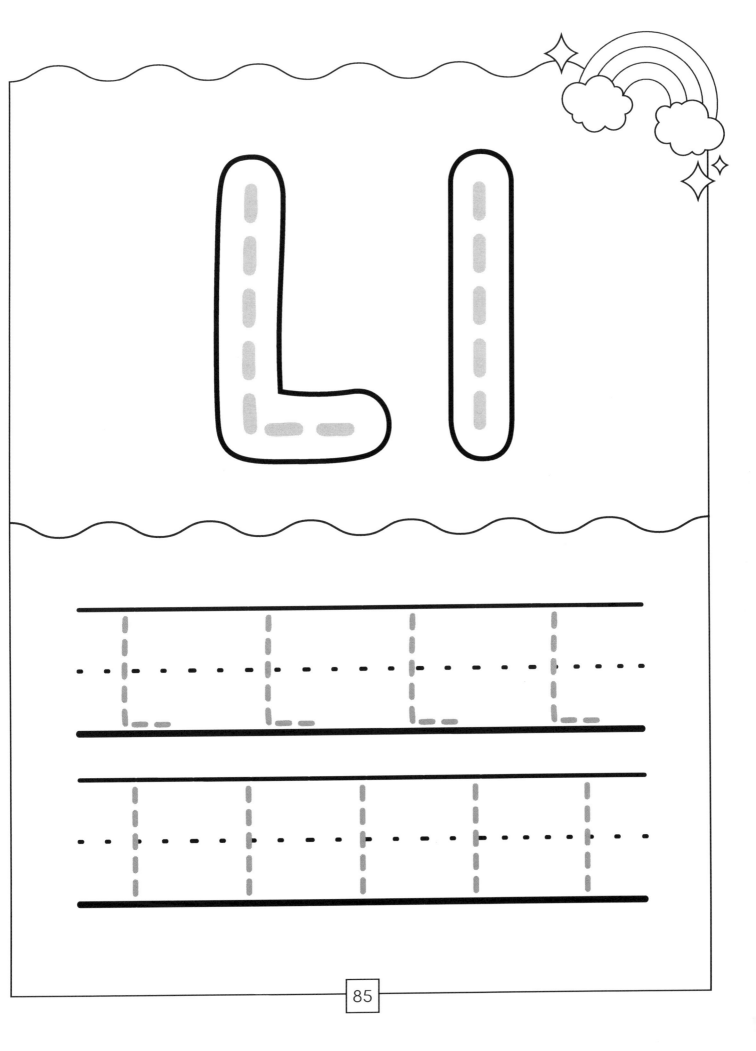

M m

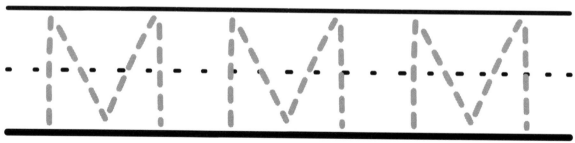

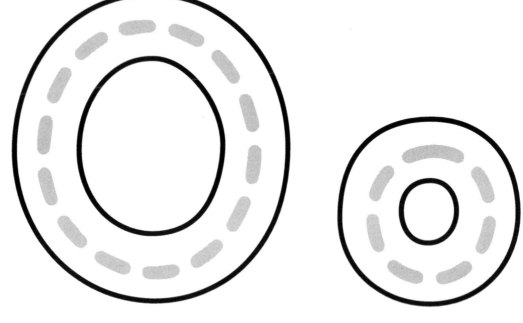

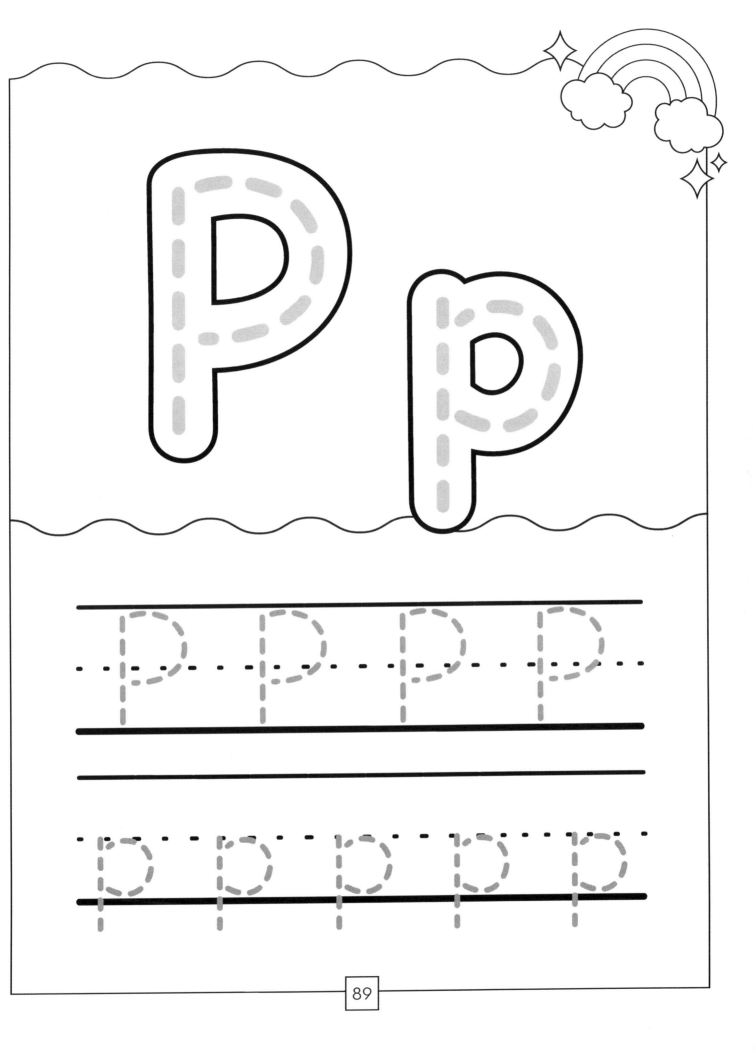

Q q

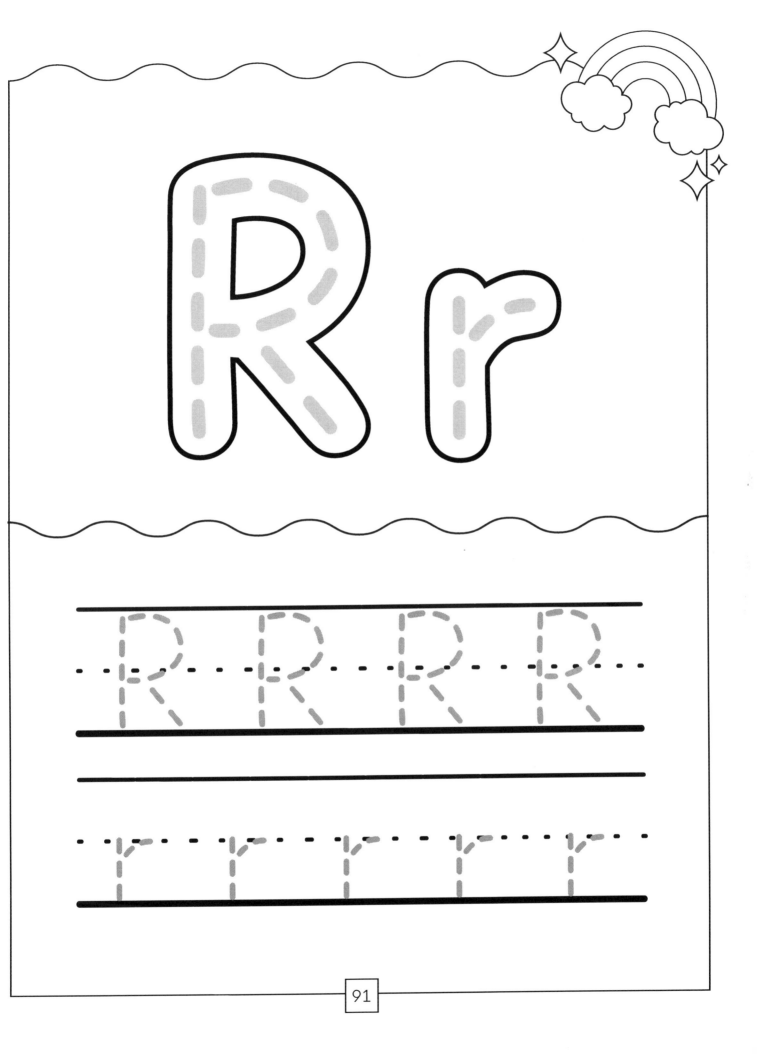

S s

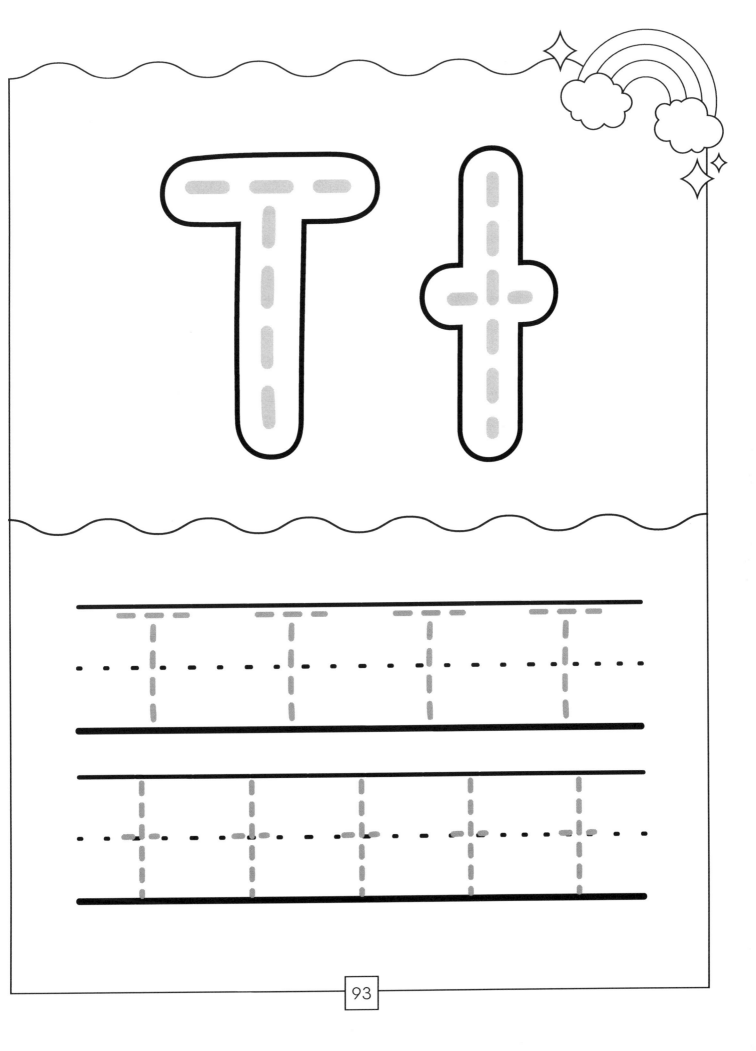

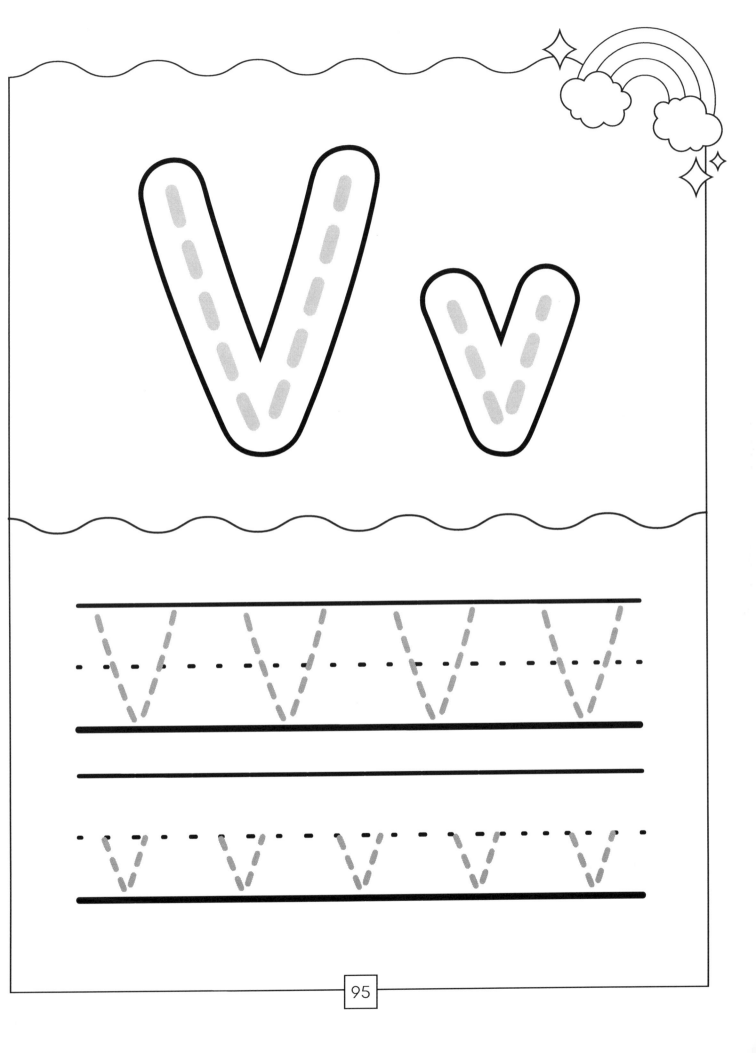

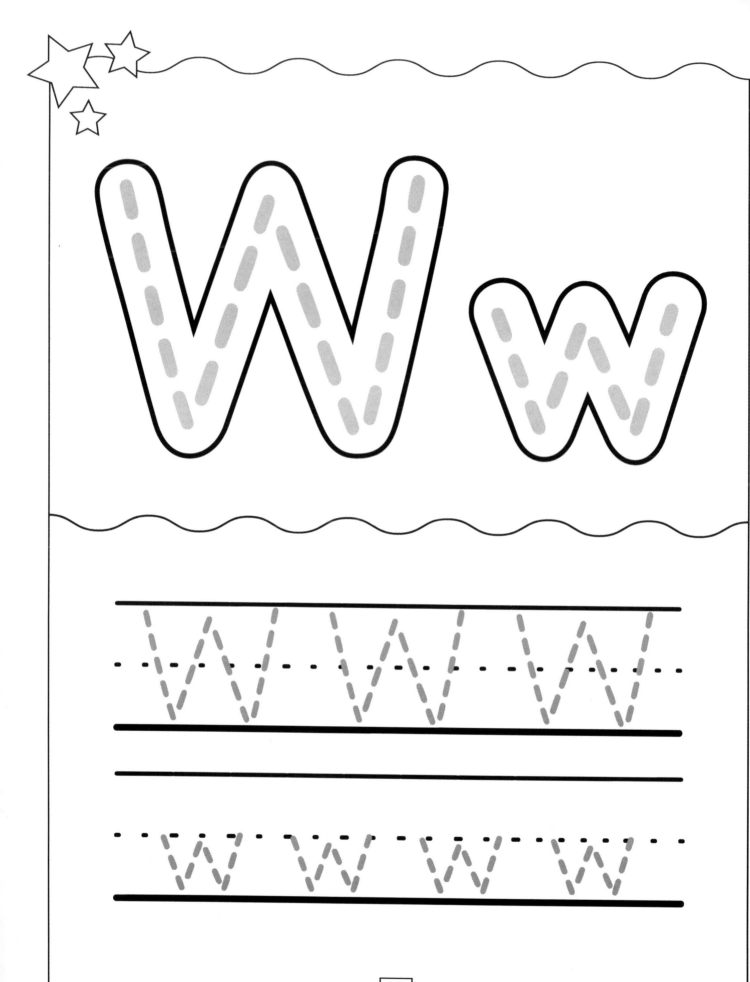

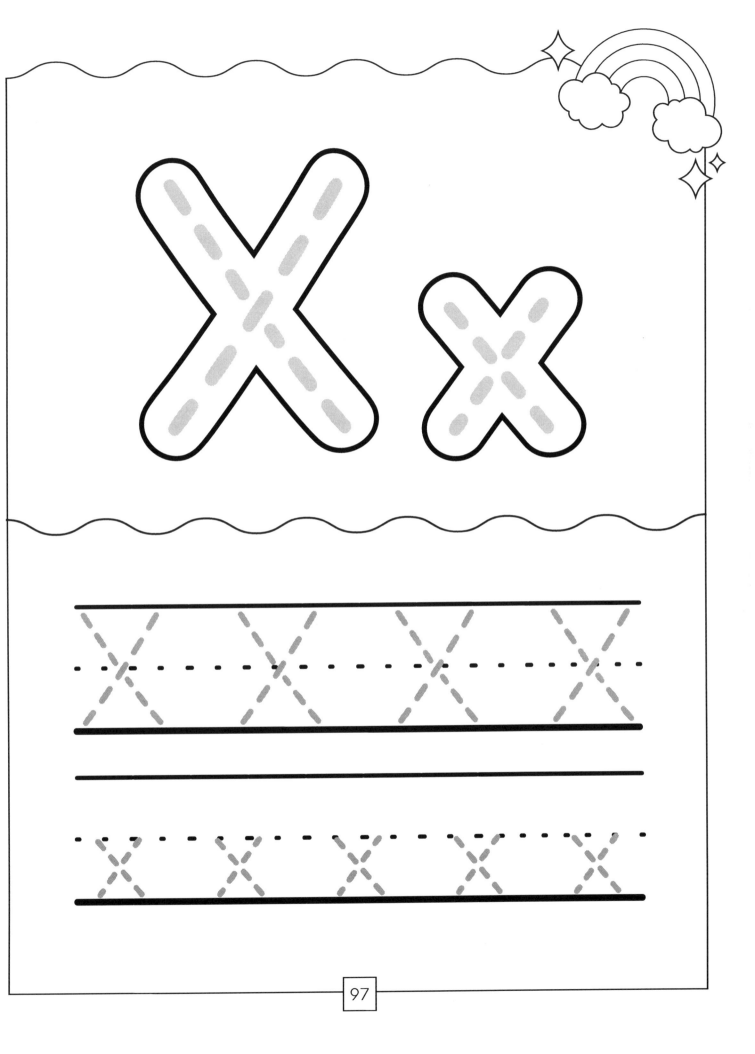

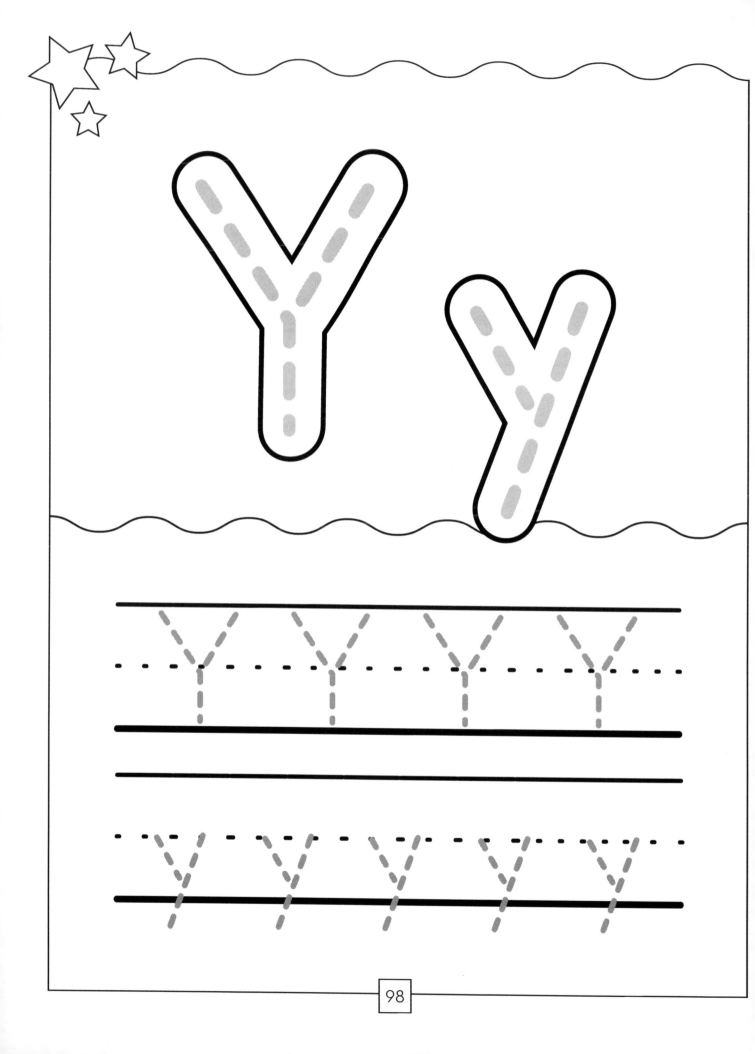

Printed in Great Britain
by Amazon